OFF-OFF-BROADWAY FESTIVAL PLAYS
(Twenty-Fifth Series)

Selected by New York theatre critics, professionals, and the editorial staff of Samuel French, Inc. as the most important plays of the Twenty-fifth Annual Off-Off-Broadway Original Short Play Festival, sponsored by Love Creek Productions.

STRAWBERRY FIELDS
by Kevin Brofsky

SIX INCH ADJUSTABLE
by Stuart Warmflash

EVENING EDUCATION
by Jeffery Scott Elwell

HOT ROD
by Jeremy Kareken

A PINK CADILLAC NIGHTMARE
by Le Wilhelm

EAST OF THE SUN
AND WEST OF THE MOON
by Peter Handy

SAMUEL FRENCH, INC.
45 West 25th Street, New York 10010-2751
7623 Sunset Blvd., Hollywood 90046-2795

IMPORTANT BILLING AND CREDIT REQUIREMENTS

All producers of STRAWBERRY FIELDS, SIX INCH ADJUSTABLE, EVENING EDUCATION, HOT ROD, A PINK CADILLAC NIGHTMARE and EAST OF THE SUN AND WEST OF THE MOON must give credit to the Author(s) of the Play(s) in all programs distributed in connection with performances of the Play(s) and in all instances in which the title (s) of the Play(s) appears for purposes of advertising, publicizing or otherwise exploiting the Play(s) and/or a production. The name of the Author *must* also appear on a separate line, on which no other name appears, immediately following the title, and *must* appear in size of type not less than fifty percent the size of the title type.

TABLE OF CONTENTS

STRAWBERRY FIELDS

by

Kevin Brofsky

Dedicated to Ed Rollins

STRAWBERRY FIELDS was presented at the Off-Off-Broadway Original Short Play Festival on June 17-18, 2000, under the direction of Derek Jamison with the following cast:

WAITRESS . . . . Rachel Permann

EDITH WARREN . . . . Susan Finch

VERA SAMUELS . . . . Rebecca Hoodwin

ABOUT THE AUTHOR

KEVIN BROFSKY has been writing plays for over twenty years. Full-length plays seen in New York include *The Matinee Ladies* and *Stars,* winner of the 1999 OOBR Award. He also wrote the book for the musical *Northern Boulevard* which starred Rosetta leNoire at AMAS Theater. Called "New York's Most Produced Playwright," Kevin Brofsky seldom has four months go by without one of his plays being staged in New York, Los Angeles or elsewhere. Among his nearly fifty one-acts are *The Heart of Texas, Shvesters, The Morning Sun* and *When My Love Comes Along*, a winner of the Turnip One-act Festival.

CHARACTERS

EDITH WARREN: mid 40s
WAITRESS: early 40s
VERA SAMUELS: early 40s

SETTING

Place: A restaurant in Plant City, Florida
Time: Present

(A table in a diner, Plant City, Florida, between Tampa and Orlando, set for two.)
(EDITH WARREN sits nervously at the table. In her mid-40s, quickly losing her looks, she wears a printed dress in an attempt to look brighter. She carries a small purse. She will speak in a southern accent.)
(A WAITRESS crosses to the table, a few years younger, somewhat tired. It's been a long day.)

WAITRESS. *(In a lower class southern accent.)* Care to see the menu, hon?
EDITH. Just strawberry shortcake and coffee, please.
WAITRESS. All righty.

(She starts to remove the setting opposite EDITH.)

EDITH. Oh, someone will be joining me.
WAITRESS. All righty. Do you want me to hold your order then?
EDITH. No … She may be running late.
WAITRESS. All righty. Pardon me, but don't I know you?
EDITH. I don't think so?
WAITRESS. You look familiar.
EDITH. I just have one of those faces, I suppose.
WAITRESS. Well, I'll go fetch your order.

(She exits. EDITH looks around, opens her purse, takes out a compact and looks at herself in the mirror.)
(VERA SAMUELS enters, as glamorous as EDITH is plain. She is a few years younger. She wears a plain tailored suit, sunglasses and a scarf covers her head.)

VERA. Ms. Warren?
EDITH. *(Jumps)* Oh! Hello!
VERA. *(Indicates the chair.)* May I … ?
EDITH. Please.

(VERA sits at the table.)

VERA. First, I want to thank you for seeing me.
EDITH. I'm sorry it couldn't have been more … I'm sure you're used to places a bit more …

VERA. You'd be surprised at some of the places I've been in, Ms. Warren. May I call you Edith? *(EDITH nods.)* I promise to make this as painless as possible. I know you've had enough to last you —
EDITH. The rest of my life.
VERA. I'm sure.

(The WAITRESS crosses to the table.)

WAITRESS. Care to see a menu, hon?
VERA. *(To EDITH.)* What are you having?
EDITH. Just strawberry shortcake and coffee.
VERA. That sounds good. *(To the WAITRESS.)* I'll have the same, please.
WAITRESS. All righty.

(She exits.)

VERA. Well, there goes my diet.
EDITH. *(To VERA.)* We're famous for our strawberry shortcake in these parts.
VERA. Yes, I saw the signs: *STRAWBERRY CAPITAL OF THE WORLD.* Is that true?
EDITH. I hope so, or Plant City wasted a lot of money putting up those signs. *(She laughs nervously.)* I'm sorry … I've never talked to anyone famous before.
VERA. A lot of people feel that way at first. That's why this meeting is so important. I want you to think of us as two friends just having a chat over strawberry shortcake. I want to assure you that the network will do everything to make sure you are treated with the respect you deserve.
EDITH. Thank you, but I want to talk with you about something.
VERA. You're not backing out, are you?
EDITH. Well, no, not really. It's just that … I don't want you to show my face.
VERA. What?
EDITH. I've thought it over and I want you to scramble my face. Like they do on *Cops.* Can you do that?
VERA. Uhhh, we can, but I thought —
EDITH. Because I'm going to tell Dave, my husband, that I'm visiting my sister up in Atlanta. And I'm calling my sister so she backs up my story in case he calls … I'm willing to go through all of that. I want them to scramble my face.
VERA. It's just that people might think you're hiding.
EDITH. I *am* hiding. I know when I called your show, I said I was ready to be interviewed, but afterwards, I thought about all it was going to involve and … Dave … I mean, suppose Dave happens to turn on the set and there I am with you when I'm supposed to be up in Atlanta with my sister?

VERA. Won't he recognize the story?

EDITH. Oh, he won't continue to watch it! Two women talking on television ... Unless he sees my face.

VERA. I understand. I want you to know I appreciate you going through all this. Millions of people across this country appreciate it, Edith.

EDITH. Thank you, Miss Samuels.

VERA. Call me Vera.

EDITH. Oh, I don't think I could do that. After all, we're not friends.

VERA. Yes, well ... Maybe we can change that today. Now, if it will make it easier for you, we can do the interview from our station in Tampa.

EDITH. No, no, I want to do it in New York ... I don't think I could do it here ... in Florida ... I just couldn't walk out afterwards and get in the car and come home. It's better if I'm somewhere foreign.

VERA. Well, there's no place more foreign than New York. *(She laughs a little.)* Don't you worry though. My producers have agreed to put you up at the Plaza Hotel complete with room and limousine service.

EDITH. I wouldn't know what to do with room service, Miss Samuels.

VERA. You'll figure it out.

EDITH. So, you're going to scramble my face?

VERA. I'm going to have to check with the producers. I must tell you though, I'm a bit disappointed.

EDITH. I imagine you know how I feel.

(She indicates VERA's sunglasses.)

VERA. *(Taking them off.)* I didn't think they would stand out in Florida.

EDITH. This is Plant City, not Palm Beach.

(The WAITRESS enters with two dishes of shortbread and two coffees on a tray.)

WAITRESS. All righty.

(She serves them and takes a moment to look at VERA without the glasses.)

VERA. Thank you.

WAITRESS. Pardon me, hon, maybe it's the day, but ev'rybody's lookin' rather familiar to me. Don't I know you from someplace?

VERA. *(Whispers)* I'm Vera Samuels.

WAITRESS. Did we go to high school together or something?

VERA. No, I'm just visiting.

WAITRESS. Oh. Well, hon, get a taste of that strawberry shortcake. Plant City ain't much, but we grow the best strawberries on earth.

(VERA hesitates a moment, then takes a bite of her shortcake.)

VERA. Oh, this is good.

WAITRESS. My granddaddy, before the Great Depression, had the biggest strawberry fields in Hillsborough County. You might say those little fruits are in my blood. Enjoy it now.

VERA. Thank you.

(The WAITRESS exits. VERA turns back to EDITH.)

EDITH. I guess she doesn't get to see too much daytime T.V.

VERA. Let me tell you about having your face on television, Edith. People for the most part do not really see who they're looking at. No one is expecting to see a television talk-show hostess sitting in a diner in Plant City, Florida. Now, if I'm trotting down the halls of Rockefeller Center or lunching at "21" or getting out of a limo at a premier, people are ready to see a celebrity, but not here. Believe me when I tell you, Edith, you'll be safe.

EDITH. You're not from a small town, are you, Miss Samuels?

VERA. Born seven blocks from the Empire State Building.

EDITH. You ever hear of small town gossip?

VERA. Of course.

EDITH. Plant City invented it.

VERA. Yes, I'll —

(The WAITRESS suddenly runs on.)

WAITRESS. VERA SAMUELS!

VERA. Yes?

WAITRESS. You're Vera Samuels ain't you?

VERA. Yes, I am.

WAITRESS. Oh, my! My! Vera Samuels in *my* restaurant! Who's gonna believe it!? Vera Samuels of *America Life*! Miss Samuels, can I have your autograph?

VERA. Of course.

WAITRESS. Here, use this!

(She gives her the order pad.)

VERA. What do you want me to write?

WAITRESS. Oh, just your name and the date. I'll frame it and hang it up over the cash register. I was in a restaurant on Collins Avenue in Miami Beach once and they had a photograph of Burt Reynolds and Dinah Shore over the … You don't happen to have a photograph of yourself, do you?

VERA. I'll tell you what, when I get back to New York, I'll have one sent to you.

WAITRESS. Oh, that would be awesome. Wait till I go tell Dapper who's eating his shortcake! He's gonna bust a gut ... Dapper's our chief.

VERA. So I gather.

WAITRESS. We call him Dapper 'cause ... *(She looks at EDITH darkly.)* You're Edith Warren, ain't you? *(EDITH nods. She turns to VERA.)* You're here to interview her, ain't you?

VERA. We're just discussing a possible interview.

WAITRESS. I don't want no trouble here ... I'm sorry, but there was never any trouble till ... We had all these reporters coming here from Tampa and Miami and now New York and San Francisco like we're a bunch of no-good klan members or something. Let me tell you something, Miss Samuels, Plant City never had no klan here, you can quote me. *(To EDITH.)* I have to drive past those strawberry fields ev'ry day and ev'ry day, what happened to your boy enters my mind. *(To VERA.)* We are people with a conscious here. I'm tired of ev'rybody talkin' like we're a bunch of rednecks. And the next time I hear talk of a conspiracy, *I'm* gonna beat somebody to a pulp.

VERA. I'm sure you're right, Ma'am.

WAITRESS. He just picked on the wrong boys, that's all. You gonna play that game, you gotta expect things like this can happen. And another thing, the ones who did it, they were from Frostproof. That's way over in Polk County. You can forget the photograph, Miss Samuels. I don't want to be reminded of why you came to Plant City.

(She exits.)

EDITH. *(To VERA.)* That's why I need my face to be scrambled.

VERA. I'm sorry. I should've known better.

EDITH. That's just the tip of the iceberg, Miss Samuels. All this fuss over my Michael ... It isn't right. He's dead. He can't hurt anyone now.

(VERA touches her hand.)

VERA. I lost my son in a car accident in 1993.

EDITH. I know you did. That's why I called your show. Both Barbara Walters and Oprah offered me more money, but I knew that you ... Well, that you knew what it felt like to lose a child. I just don't know if I should go through with it, that's all. I mean, what's it going to do? Stop people from hating?

VERA. I just wanted to put a face on this.

EDITH. My boy's face was in every newspaper in the country.

VERA. I wanted to show my viewers that he was loved. Right now, Michael Warren is just a symbol. The young man who got himself hurt because of what he was. Edith, most people in this county don't march down streets in protest. Most people in this country don't beat people to death. Most people just sit at home and watch the news and tell themselves "how awful," eat dinner and go to bed. They have no thought that their ... son, their daughter could be next. Nothing will change unless the victims stand up and say "No!"

EDITH. I was never meant to change the world, Miss Samuels. I know what you're saying, Miss Samuels. I grew up in the south in the '60s after all. I didn't march for civil rights, but that didn't mean I didn't empathize.

VERA. Of course you did. Did you have many black friends, Edith?

EDITH. I ... No .. Atlanta was rather ... segregated then. I was a kid.

VERA. Do you have any gay friends, Edith?

EDITH. This is a small town, Miss Samuels. We don't go around ... We just don't discuss certain things. I guess that's why I'm having a problem here. I just wasn't brought up to discuss certain things.

VERA. But you knew ... about Michael, didn't you?

EDITH. Oh, I guess everybody knew ... Michael was ... You know, he was born prematurely-maturely ... *(Laughs nervously.)* He was such a little guy. He used to tell people he was five feet tall. He was four-eleven and a half. He would always wear these platforms ... He used to say, "being a short man in America is just hell" ... He never had an easy time of it. I guess a lot of folks made remarks. He never went into sports or anything and down here, that's a sin next to not going to Sunday service ... Dave, my husband, more or less ignored him ... Used to call him a ... even before ... When he told me he met a boy at the Rollands College, up in Winter Park, I was kinda happy for him. I mean, Michael was always sorta ... a loner, you know. I thought he was finally making his own way ... *(She starts to break down.)* I'm sorry, Miss Samuels, I don't think I can do the interview. I don't want to do this on television. I'm sorry I wasted everyone's time.

(She stands.)

VERA. Please, Edith ... My son wasn't killed in an automobile accident. *(EDITH stares at her.)* That's the story we gave to the media. The truth was ... He was crossing Fourteenth Street in New York and some boys in a car ... Witnesses said they called his name and ran into him ... Just picked him out of the crowd and kept on going. The car hit him with such force ... He died instantly.

EDITH. Then we are the same.

VERA. Yes.

EDITH. Then *you* should tell *your* story, Miss Samuels.

VERA. I can't, Edith. I'm a celebrity.

EDITH. And you don't want to risk the ridicule.

VERA. I can't.

EDITH. Shouldn't it be the mothers of the boys who killed our sons facing the ridicule? Why aren't we proud of our sons?

VERA. I was proud.

EDITH. Not enough to risk your reputation with the public. You want me to do it for you.

VERA. No, Edith.

EDITH. *(Sitting)* I will make a deal with you, Miss Samuels. I will go on *America Life* and talk about my son, if you will talk about yours.

VERA. I can't.

EDITH. Then I can't come on your show.

VERA. You're asking me to do something —

EDITH. I'm asking you to do only what you're asking me. "I'm a celebrity," you said. You have to live with the consequences. Well, so do I. I have to come back here and live in this town and live with my husband and live with the consequences, just like you ... But we have to stand up for our sons. They can't do it for themselves.

(The WAITRESS returns.)

WAITRESS. *(Coldly)* Will there be anything else?

VERA. Yes, please, I would like an apology.

WAITRESS. I beg your —

VERA. I feel as though you insulted my friend Miss Warren and me for no reason.

WAITRESS. I haven't done any such —

VERA. Yes, you did. As soon as you found out who we are, you insulted us. That is called prejudice, Miss, and we expect an apology.

WAITRESS. Do you want me to get Dapper?

VERA. No, I want you to apologize for your behavior.

(Outraged, the WAITRESS adds up the bill, tears it off and slams it on the table.)

WAITRESS. Please do me the favor and *don't* leave me a tip.

VERA. Oh, I don't think there's any reason to worry over that.

WAITRESS. I want you to leave now. I'll call Dapper. I'll call the *poleese* if I have to.

VERA. And what would you tell the *po-leese*?

(An awkward pause. The WAITRESS has some difficulties making up a reason.)

WAITRESS. You are creatin' a disturbance. A *public* disturbance.

VERA. No, we're not. We're just two women sitting at a table eating strawberry shortcake. We're not disturbing anyone. What is *disturbed* is in *your* head, Ma'am. This is a public establishment and *we* have every right to be here! *(The WAITRESS looks at them and exits. VERA rises and goes towards the kitchen.)* Don't you walk away from us! I demand that you come back here and explain yourself! I want to know what makes you hate! ... *(More or less to herself.)* What gives you the right to hate ... people you don't even know.

EDITH. *(Amazed)* My heavens, nobody ever talks like that in public down here.

VERA. Oh, in New York, it's a daily occurrence.

(They look at each other and start to laugh.)

EDITH. It does make you angry, doesn't it?

VERA. It's like being kicked in the teeth.

EDITH. No, it's like being kicked in the heart. *(Stands, takes the bill.)* Let's get out of here. Vera, about the show ...

VERA. We have to come out together, don't we? For Michael and Jacob.

EDITH. Jacob, that's a nice name.

VERA. Yes, it is.

(She takes EDITH's arm and they stroll out together as the lights fade to black.)

END OF PLAY

COSTUME PLOT

EDITH:
Plain printed summer housedress (something a poor southern woman might think she looks good in), earrings, flat shoes

VERA:
Solid-colored tailored summer-wear (from the best Fifth Avenue stores), earrings, high-heels

WAITRESS:
Bright T-shirt, jeans, apron (optional)

PROPERTY PLOT

2 Pie plates
2 Sets of knives
2 Sets of forks
2 Paper napkins
2 Coffee cups (or mugs)
2 Slices strawberry shortcake (sponge cake / whipped cream / strawberries)
Creamer container
Sugar container
Waitress pad
Pen

SIX INCH ADJUSTABLE

by
Stuart Warmflash

*Six Inch Adjustable would not have been possible
without the on-going support and encouragement
from my beloved wife Julie,
my dedicated family of colleagues at The Harbor Theatre,
and the contributions of time, talent and insight
of the two actors,
Vinnie Sagona and Erik Van Wyck.*

SIX INCH ADJUSTABLE was presented at the Off-Off-Broadway Original Short Play Festival on July 11th and July 16th, 2000, under the direction of Stuart Warmflash with the following cast:

CHIP . . . . .Vinnie Sagona

TUDIE . . . . Erik Van Wyck

ABOUT THE AUTHOR

A native New Yorker, STUART WARMFLASH has been involved with the theatre for over thirty years. After graduating from NYU he attended the Central School of Speech and Drama in London (1971-74). Subsequently he enjoyed a successful acting career, appearing on Broadway (with the distinguished APA-Phoenix Repertory Co.), Off-Broadway and regionally, as well as in film and television. His first play, *Art's Life,* played an extended run on Theatre Row and his subsequent works have been read and/or performed in and outside of New York. *Lost at Sea* won two National Play Contests including the New Play Festival at the Charlotte Repertory Company. *Heart-Timers* won first prize and a production at both the Theatre-in-the-Works contest (Amherst, MA) and the Festival of Emerging American Theatre contest at the Equity Phoenix Theatre in Indianapolis. For two and half years, Mr. Warmflash toured his acclaimed one-man show, *A Map And A Cap...* which was chosen as a semi-finalist in the Forest A. Roberts/Shiras Institute Competition. *Owning the Knuckleball*, developed at the Eugene O'Neill Theater Center, was produced in London. More recent works include *Together Tulane, Bizet's Locket* (winner of the Paul Green and Riverside Stage Awards), and *The Czar of Nothingness*. His award-winning full-length documentary entitled "Unforgotten: Willowbrook 25 Years Later" opened to excellent reviews both in Los Angeles and New York. Mr. Warmflash is the artistic director of The Harbor Theatre, a seven-year-old non-profit collective of seven playwrights and thirty actors and directors. The company has produced several full-length plays, an annual one-act festival and sponsored public readings of members' works. He is a member of the Dramatist Guild, AEA, AFTRA and SAG.

CHARACTERS

CHIP: A 21 year old, upstate college student
TUDIE: His 15 year old brother

SETTING

Place: A suburban driveway
Time: Present

(A Long Island suburban driveway. Unusually warm Thanksgiving Sunday.)

(CHIP, 21, is re-assembling portions of his brother TUDIE's, 15, motorcycle engine, a messy job.)

TUDIE. Still can't believe I got it for 50 bucks. A Triumph cycle for 50 bucks. Amazing, huh? 'N did I tell ya? The guy said his wife MADE him get rid of it.

CHIP. Happens all the time. Hand me that rag.

TUDIE. *(Beat, then.)* Hey, Chip? You think I can come up and visit you at school?

CHIP. We'll see.

TUDIE. Mom said I could go after New Years. She's talking about going away somewhere with Aunt Frannie in January.

CHIP. With Aunt Frannie? She told you that?

TUDIE. Yeah. She's gotta go with someone, doesn't she? Why?

CHIP. No reason. So why am I changing the rings?

TUDIE. 'Cause they were cracked.

CHIP. Yeah, but what happens when they're cracked?

TUDIE. You lose compression, the oil leaks down the piston into the cylinder and the exhaust blows blue.

CHIP. Good. Hand me the six-inch adjustable.

TUDIE. Which is … ?

CHIP. "Which is?" There's only one that's six inches.

TUDIE. This one?

CHIP. Yeah. *(Takes it.)* Best all around tool in the box. Dozens of times this baby saved me one way or another.

(Silence as CHIP uses it to tighten an engine mount.)

TUDIE. Chip, how can you be sure when we put all this back together that it's gonna run?

CHIP. What?

TUDIE. When we put it all together. Suppose it doesn't start?

CHIP. Then I'll take it apart and check everything.

TUDIE. Then what?

CHIP. What do you mean, "Then what?" Then it'll start.

TUDIE. Suppose it doesn't? I mean, suppose the guy who sold it to me knew that there was something really wrong with it and —

CHIP. It'll start, Tudie … Hand me the calibrator.

TUDIE. The thing with the … ?

19

CHIP. This, here! *(Grabs it.)* Jesus, how the hell are you ever going to learn to fix anything if you don't even know the tools, huh?

TUDIE. *(Overlapping)* I knew, I knew.

CHIP. You think I'm gonna come racing home with my kit every time you get dirt in the carburetor or a vapor lock in the fuel line?

TUDIE. No. I'll save up and get a set.

CHIP. You do that. Save every penny 'cause a decent tool kit these days costs, like 500 bucks .. What the hell was I doing?

TUDIE. The calibrator.

CHIP. Oh, yeah. Toss me that manual.

TUDIE. *(Does, beat, then.)* Can I do something?

CHIP. Not this sec.

TUDIE. *(Half to himself.)* You're like, doing everything ... *(Beat, then.)* How're your roommates doing?

CHIP. They're all right.

TUDIE. God, it must be so cool having your own place, being able to do whatever you want, anytime you want. Close your door and no one can bug the hell outta you.

CHIP. All right, hand me the plugs.

TUDIE. You, like, stay up all night, sometimes, right?

CHIP. Look, do you want your bike running or not?

TUDIE. Yeah, of course!

CHIP. Then pay attention. What am I gonna do with this calibrator?

TUDIE. Calibrate.

CHIP. Don't be a smart-ass. Calibrate what?

TUDIE. The spark-plugs. I'm not stupid.

CHIP. No one said you were. But there's more to it, see. The gap's too wide, the plug won't fire. Too small, no good. And if it's off even one-hundredths of an inch, the timing'll be shot to hell and then what?

TUDIE. It'll sputter and cough and I'll look like a total jerk stalling out in the middle of town.

CHIP. No you won't cause it's not gonna stall out. Now, besides, calibrating, the other thing to make sure of with the plugs is what?

TUDIE. That they're clean.

CHIP. Good boy. Here. Here's a rag. Use that gasoline to clean 'em up.

(TUDIE cleans the spark plugs with the gasoline and rag while CHIP wipes his hands and flips through pages of the manual.)

TUDIE. The guy wanted 100 bucks but I told him all I had was 50. You think I got a good deal, right?

CHIP. I think you shoulda got your driver's license first.

TUDIE. Oh, another 13 weeks 'n I'll have it. And I can always ride it out on the dirt flats til then.

CHIP. Great. You take a spill and sure as shit, mom'll be on my ass.

TUDIE. Hey, I'll be careful.

CHIP. *(Flipping pages.)* Dumb manual doesn't …

TUDIE. *(Beat)* Is Elissa coming over later?

CHIP. No.

TUDIE. When we're done here, can we go for a ride? Test 'er out?

CHIP. Yeah, all right.

TUDIE. Cool. We could open 'er up out on Lloyd's Neck 'n maybe then swing by Elissa's and show her what a great job you did fixing 'er up.

CHIP. Won't be time.

TUDIE. But you said you don't have to start heading back to school until eight o'clock or so.

CHIP. Yeah, but I got things to do.

TUDIE. Oh. You and Elissa, you wanna be together and all. Yeah, I understand, Chip. That's cool.

CHIP. Tudie, just concentrate on what's in front of us, all right? Shit!

TUDIE. Sorry. What did I say?

CHIP. You're worrying about all kinds of shit you shouldn't be thinking about, huh? Just pay attention to what's in front of you and everything'll work out, OK? OK?

TUDIE. OK.

CHIP. *(Re: manual.)* God damn chart doesn't say …

TUDIE. *(Spark plug.)* This all right?

CHIP. Does it look all right? *(Pointing)* There's still all that carbon crap here.

TUDIE. Oh, yeah.

CHIP. What ya gotta do now is file it. Carefully. Here, watch. *(CHIP slowly strokes the file over the spark plug head.)* See, takes all the crap off. But don't file it down too much or —

TUDIE. It won't fire.

CHIP. Right.

(TUDIE works silently. CHIP takes inventory of the parts surrounding him.)

TUDIE. Know what, Chip? Next summer we'll both have motorcycles. You'll be managing the print shop for Uncle Hack and, did I tell ya? He said I could work there, too. Just sweeping up, but still, it'll be a paycheck.

CHIP. *(Looks long and hard at TUDIE, then.)* Tudie.

TUDIE. *(Not looking up.)* Yeah?

CHIP. How're you doing in school?

TUDIE. Awright. *(Beat, then.)* Why?

CHIP. Just … Mom's buggin' me, is all.

TUDIE. I'm doing fine.

CHIP. What about sports. Didn't you try out for the soccer team?

TUDIE. Yeah.

CHIP. What happened?

TUDIE. Asshole Breuner.

CHIP. He cut you?

TUDIE. Yeah. I played great, too. At the try-outs? Three perfect goal kicks in a row. Whizzed right past Roger Canby and Fuentes headed them right in. And I dribbled the figure 8's in like, 10 seconds. So it's his God damn loss.

CHIP. Yeah, well, don't take it too hard. He wasn't crazy about me either.

TUDIE. Breuner? Yeah, but you were so good he couldn't get rid of you, right?

CHIP. Tudie, no one's that good, understand? He could've gotten rid of me easy.

TUDIE. So why didn't he, if he didn't like you?

CHIP. Because … hell, I dunno, I never gave him a good excuse.

TUDIE. What are you saying?

CHIP. He's an asshole but if you were playing good he wouldn't just — what did you do?

TUDIE. I didn't do anything.

CHIP. Nothing? You didn't do something to piss him off?

TUDIE. I called him "Frank".

CHIP. What?! What the fuck did you do that for!?

TUDIE. I don't KNOW! I was feeling good, some of the older kids were calling him —

CHIP. Not to his face! No one calls him Frank to his face, he hates that! Jesus, Tudie.

(CHIP flips through the manual.)

TUDIE. *(Beat, then.)* Mom, say anything else to you?

CHIP. 'Bout what?

TUDIE. 'Bout me.

CHIP. Not much.

TUDIE. I bet. She probably told you I'm not talking to her. Or to my teachers or much of anyone else, right?

CHIP. No.

TUDIE. She grills me all the time. How come I'm not hangin' out with Richie or Phil anymore? How come I'm not doing my homework? How come I'm spending 90 hours a day in the basement watching TV and reading MotorCycle World. How come this, how come that. What does she think, I'm plotting an assassination or something?

CHIP. She's got stuff on her mind.

TUDIE. Yeah. So what did she say to you?

CHIP. Nothing, Tudie. I hardly talk to her myself, all right? You finish with those spark plugs, yet?

TUDIE. Yeah.

CHIP. Good. *(Using the socket wrench, CHIP screws one of them into the engine block. TUDIE stands watching enviously. After a moment CHIP turns to him.)* All right, you put this one in.

TUDIE. *(Can I?)* Yeah?

CHIP. It's your bike, isn't it? Here. *(CHIP puts the spark plug in the socket wrench for TUDIE who starts screwing it in.)* OK, good. Go easy, now. *(TUDIE turns it slowly with deliberate intent.)* What are you performing surgery? *(TUDIE moves more rapidly, tightening it down.)* Good. Now, not too tight or —

(The spark plug's head snaps off.)

TUDIE. Uh-oh.

CHIP. Wha — ? Oh FUCK! FuckfuckfuckfuckfuckfuckfuckFUCK!!!

TUDIE. *(Helpless)* I'm … sorry.

CHIP. SON OF A FUCKING BITCH!!!

TUDIE. I'm sorry … We can get it out, right?

CHIP. No, not today.

TUDIE. How come?

CHIP. Because now I gotta take the whole thing apart, pull it out from the inside and —

TUDIE. Maybe we could use the six inch? You said —

CHIP. To pull a snapped spark plug? No, we can't use the God damn — We can use the six inch to dis-assemble the whole fucking engine and then, never mind.

TUDIE. *(With his hands.)* Maybe I can —

CHIP. With your hands? What are you, a moron? Leave it, Tudie, just leave it alone!

TUDIE. But you're taking off later. What am I gonna do with … ?

CHIP. Christ, that's YOUR fucking problem! I didn't buy the God damn thing.

TUDIE. Fine! I'll let it sit right here in the driveway until you come home over Christmas. Mom'll have a cow but too bad.

(TUDIE starts out. CHIP opens a bottle of beer and chugs.)

CHIP. Where're you going?

TUDIE. Basement.

CHIP. Tudie.

TUDIE. What?

(CHIP sits.)

CHIP. Come here. *(Coaxing)* Come on, have a beer.

TUDIE. I'm too young to drink.

CHIP. Not what I heard. Howie's kid sister said you were drinking with the Gilman brothers in Grace Avenue Park.

TUDIE. Yeah? Well.

CHIP. Come on, sit down. Chill out. Here. *(He pops a beer and offers it. TUDIE sits and takes a sip.)* Let me ask you something. How long you gonna be in school for?

TUDIE. What?

CHIP. How much longer are you going to be in school?

TUDIE. Shit, Chip it's only Thanksgiving. I still got months and months of —

CHIP. I mean, high school.

TUDIE. High school? What kinda dumb question is that? I'm in 10th, I got 11th and 12th to go. Any moron can figure that out. What are you asking me?

CHIP. Then what?

TUDIE. Then what, what? God, you sound like Amanato, my guidance counselor with the braided nose-hairs. Then what? How should I know? I guess I'll go to some dumb-ass college what difference does it make?

CHIP. But it's only another couple of years, right?

TUDIE. Unless I drop out.

CHIP. You won't drop out. You're too smart to do something that dumb.

TUDIE. And you think it's dumb to drop out.

CHIP. Yes, I do ... So you're around another two and a half years and then you're off to college where you're not gonna screw up like me, right?

TUDIE. *(Realizes, statement.)* You're not gonna have enough credits to graduate in the spring, are you?

CHIP. *(Ignoring him.)* So you'll go off to college and what about Mom?

TUDIE. What about her?

CHIP. You're gonna be outta the house. How's she gonna manage?

TUDIE. She's got a job, the house is, like, paid off. What are you talking about?

CHIP. I'm talking about her and Chester.

TUDIE. Chester?

CHIP. Don't play dumb. Mom's friend, Chester.

TUDIE. *(Laughs hard.)* Oh, Ches-ter! Jesus, Chip, the guy's so pathetic. Takes him 10 minutes to have a thought and another twenty to get it out. *(Imitating)* "Ah, ah, ah, Tudie ... Ah, ah, ah how's, ah, school?" *(Laughs again.)* And his teeth? The guy's a dentist and he's got teeth like a camel. Good thing he's way out in Jersey.

CHIP. The thing is, mom kinda likes him.

TUDIE. Oh, right. I don't think so.

CHIP. You're wrong.

TUDIE. What the hell do you know, you're 200 miles away.

CHIP. I know she's not going away with Aunt Frannie. And I know she's thinking about going off with Chester for a few days.

TUDIE. Mom?! With Chester? You're full a shit.

CHIP. Tudie, whether you like it or —

(TUDIE knocks the beer can out of CHIP's hands.)

TUDIE. Fuck you, she woulda told me!

CHIP. Tudie —

TUDIE. No! Mom never — with Chester, I mean, that's a joke! What are you telling me this crap for?

CHIP. Fine. I don't know what I'm talking about.

TUDIE. Mom told you this?

CHIP. Look, it doesn't matter.

TUDIE. What d'ya mean it doesn't matter! Dad's fucking dead less 'n a year and you're telling me she's fucking Chester and it doesn't —

(CHIP slaps him hard.)

CHIP. Don't you use that fucking language around me, you hear? *(TUDIE stares flabbergasted. A moment.)* Listen to me. It's not about Chester, it's about Mom. Even if she doesn't go away with him, at some point she's gonna wanna go away with someone. Somewhere. And I'm not talking about Aunt Frannie, get it? And she should have the right to do what she wants.

TUDIE. So she did speak to you.

CHIP. Well, yeah, but not about all this.

TUDIE. What'd she say?

CHIP. She's worried about you. See, I'm outta the house and don't come home all that much ...

TUDIE. No shit, Sherlock. But I don't blame you. I mean, that's why getting these wheels, I could come up to you and you wouldn't have to deal with mom ragging on you the way she does.

CHIP. She's got her reasons. I mean, she's had it real hard since Dad. We all have.

TUDIE. At least, you didn't have to watch him keel over ...

CHIP. I know. If I coulda been here, believe me. But I was at school and that's the way it is. Was. Anyway, another few years, you're gonna be off on your own. Mom's got the rest of her life. We don't want her going to that dumb job every day wishing she was doing something with her life, with someone, do we?

TUDIE. I didn't think about it.

CHIP. Course not. So. Say she likes this guy ...

TUDIE. *(Prompting)* Chester.

CHIP. I KNOW his name. Chester.

TUDIE. You think he's a moron, too, don't you, Chip?

CHIP. I ... I don't know.

TUDIE. Trust me, ole camel-teeth's a total moron. I wouldn't let him NEAR my mouth.

CHIP. OK, OK, say he is IS a total moron. Point is, if mom wants to marry him —

TUDIE. Marry!?

CHIP. Or anyone else, we should give her our blessings. I'm just saying ...

TUDIE. She wants to get married, she should hitch up with Gary Vernon down at the motorcycle shop. Then we'd get free parts and service ... She tell you she wanted to marry him?

CHIP. No, no, no. I don't think it's gotten that far. But it might someday.

TUDIE. So why'd she start talking about all this with you, now?

CHIP. Huh?

TUDIE. She just brought it up outta the blue? "Hey Chip, do me a favor and tell Trudie I might get married again one day"?

CHIP. No.

TUDIE. Then how'd it come up?

CHIP. I told her I'm going away.

TUDIE. She knows that. After dinner you're heading back — ... you're not going back to school.

CHIP. No.

TUDIE. Where're you going?

CHIP. Got a job offer managing an auto shop in Troy.

TUDIE. Oh. *(Long pause.)* When does it start?

CHIP. Tomorrow.

TUDIE. No more school, huh? What'd mom say?

CHIP. She had a conniption.

TUDIE. Huh. And Elissa?

CHIP. What about her?

TUDIE. I thought you and she had all these plans to ... You and she still gonna, you know, go out?

CHIP. No.

TUDIE. How come?

CHIP. Because she — None of your God damn business! It's no one's business what the hell I do or do not do! And if you weren't so fucking helpless, there wouldn't be any of this shit going down and I'd be — you want to know what mom said?! You want to know? All right I'll tell you. She said she didn't want me leaving cause of you. Going on and on about how I owe it to you to be around more and bring you up to my school all the time and I told her I don't owe you or anyone else anything. I'm not supposed to have a life because she's fucking you up, treating you like some 10 year old and I told her you need to grow up. Shit, if you weren't such a God damn basket case, no one woulda said anything.

TUDIE. You think I'm a basket case?

CHIP. You tell me! Living in the basement like a fucking hermit, talking to no one but mouthing off to coach Breuner, buying a fucking motorcycle from the Ice Age that needs, like, a month's worth of work and you don't even have any tools! Not to mention a God damn driver's license. Expecting I'm gonna come home and fix everything up for you instead of you reading the manual yourself, scrounging up a bunch a tools and doing it yourself YEAH I think you're a basket case!

TUDIE. Well, don't come home anymore. Ever. See if I care! I don't want to see your ugly face again, you fucking asshole. And I hope on the way to Troy you crash and die.

(TUDIE exits.)

CHIP. Shit.

(TUDIE enters.)

TUDIE. And if you don't crash, I hope there's a humongous earthquake 'n you and the entire shitty city get swallowed up and die! *(TUDIE exits. Beat. He enters.)* And you know what else? Elissa's better off without you.

(TUDIE exits.)

CHIP. *(Calls out.)* Fuck you!

(TUDIE enters.)

TUDIE. No, fuck you! Fuck you because, because … *(The damn breaks through heaving sobs and tears.)* Because you're right. I am a fucking basket case. A great big fucking loser. I wouldn't even want me around. So you go. Get out of this hell hole. Go have a life, even if I don't have one, you big moron. And I'm sorry Mom had to … I'm sorry I'm such a loser. *(TUDIE sits and cries. After an agonizing moment, CHIP moves to his side. Still crying.)* NO! Get away from the great big loser!

CHIP. You're not a loser, Tudie.

TUDIE. You're right, I'm not a loser. I'm a basket case loser.

CHIP. You're just going through a tough time.

TUDIE. Yeah, like my whole life.

CHIP. Come on.

TUDIE. *(Recovering)* Crying like the baby I am.

CHIP. Yeah, well, maybe you're better off getting it out that way then, like, blowing up.

TUDIE. Why?

CHIP. I donno.

TUDIE. That's stupid

CHIP. Maybe.

TUDIE. *(Long pause, then.)* I didn't mean it about you crashing. Or the earthquake.

CHIP. I didn't think you did.

TUDIE. What the hell am I going to do with this pile of junk?

CHIP. It's not a pile of junk.

TUDIE. Maybe I'll hang some Barbie dolls on it and turn it into an art project.

CHIP. *(Long beat.)* Look, this tool set is gonna be a bitch to lug all the way up to Troy. I'm gonna leave it here for you. For now.

TUDIE. But you'll need it.

CHIP. I'll get another one. No big deal.

(Both of them stare at the engine a moment. CHIP picks up the six inch adjustable to begin work.)

TUDIE. Take the whole thing apart and pull the sparkplug from the inside, huh.

CHIP. Yeah.

TUDIE. *(Long beat, then.)* Hand me the six inch.

(Lights fade.)

END OF PLAY

COSTUME PLOT

TUDIE:
> Worn blue jeans, scruffy engineering boots, open work shirt covering an "alternative band" T-shirt and a non-descript cap turned backwards

CHIP:
> Clean mechanic work pants (neatly pressed), flannel shirt over a T-shirt, sneakers

PROPERTY PLOT

One stripped-down motorcycle engine, preferably a small model
Professional-looking tool box filled with assorted car mechanic's tools
Six inch adjustable wrench
Several spark plugs (one of which is already "snapped" broken)
Ratchet and socket wrench set (for insertion and removal of spark plugs)
Calibrator (for the spark plugs)
File
Nondescript pan, (old cooking pan) to hold "gasoline" to clean spark plugs. (NOTE: Actual gasoline should not be used in production.)
Motorcycle Manual (old)
Three heavy duty plastic milk crates. One for each of the characters to sit on and one to place the motorcycle engine on
Old, large blanket used as a "drop cloth"
Two cans of beer (Budweiser)
Assorted rags

SET DRAWING

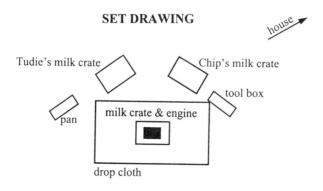

EVENING EDUCATION

by

Jeffery Scott Elwell

For Cortez Nance, Jr.,
a great friend and a great actor

EVENING EDUCATION WAS ORIGINALLY PRODUCED Off-Off-Broadway by Love Creek Productions at the Nat Horne Theatre on August 29, 1994. The cast included Cortez Nance, Jr. as Aaron.

EVENING EDUCATION was produced by Nebraska Repertory Theatre in the 2000 Off-Off-Broadway Original Short Play Festival at the American Theatre for Actors on July 14 and 15, 2000. The play was directed by Ken McCulough. Brad Buffum was production manager. William Kenyon designed the scenery and the sound. Jenny Kenyon designed the costumes. The cast was as follows:

AARON . . . . Stan Brown

TOPPMAN . . . . Kristopher Gordon Kling

ABOUT THE AUTHOR

JEFFERY SCOTT ELWELL is Professor and Chair of the Department of Theatre Arts at the University of Nebraska-Lincoln and Executive Artistic Director of the Nebraska Repertory Theatre. He received his Ph.D. from Southern Illinois University in 1986 and has a Mississippi Arts Commission Playwriting Fellowship, a Tennessee Williams Scholarship, and an NEH Summer Seminar Fellowship. Winner of numerous grants and fellowships, he has had his plays produced by professional theaters in Chicago, Los Angeles, New Orleans, New York and Lund, Sweden. Eighteen of his works have been produced Off-Off-Broadway. Published works include *Escape from Bondage, Being Frank, The Art of Dating* (in Samuel French's *Off-Off-Broadway Festival Plays, Twentieth Series), Dead Fish, Stepping Out, An Ordinary Morning,* the opening scene from *Death on a Doorstep* (in the anthology *A Grand Entrance)*, as well as two monologues in *Baseball Monologues.* An evening of his one-act plays, under the collective title of *Strained Relationships*, ran Off-Off-Broadway at the Soho Arts group in 1997 and one of the plays, *The Turn Down*, was selected for the 1998 Off-Off-Broadway Original Short Play Festival.

CHARACTERS

> STEPHEN TOPPMAN: a professor of dramatic literature
> AARON FOSTER: the night janitor at the college

SETTING

> Place: Stephen Toppman's cramped office
> Time: Evening, 6 pm

(Lights come up on the cramped office of a college professor. Upstage center are three bookcases filled with textbooks, books of literary criticism, plays and fiction. Downstage center is a professor's desk, extremely neat and furnished with the usual accessories [blotter, stapler, tape dispenser, baskets, etc.] as well as one unusual one: a gray marble obelisk serving as a paperweight. To the left of the desk are two file cabinets. To the right are two chairs, perpendicular to one another. On the back wall, are several play posters and flyers for writing programs and contests, STEPHEN TOPPMAN, a professor of dramatic literature, enters and takes a seat behind his desk. He places his satchel on the desk, opens it, and begins searching for a file. He finds it, closes the satchel, takes several sheets of notes from the file folder and begins reading through the notes. He stops and pulls a small CD player from one of the desk drawers. He turns it on and the office is filled with Mozart. From another desk drawer, he pulls out a bottle of brandy and an ornate snifter. He pours a small amount into the snifter, drinks it, and goes back to reading. There is a sudden knock at the door and TOPPMAN quickly replaces the brandy and the snifter as he answers.)

TOPPMAN. *(Closing drawer.)* You may enter. *(AARON FOSTER, an older somewhat distinguished-looking man of African-American descent, enters pulling a large trash can on wheels behind him. He is the night janitor at the college.)* Yes, Aaron. What is it?

AARON. I came to get the trash.

TOPPMAN. It hasn't moved.

AARON. Yes, sir.

(AARON goes behind the desk as TOPPMAN continues reading. He picks up the wastebasket and empties it into the larger trash can. He puts it back and then stands, not moving.)

TOPPMAN. *(Looking up.)* Is there something else?

AARON. I was hopin' I might talk to you, Mr. Toppman.

TOPPMAN. It's Doctor Toppman.

AARON. Sorry 'bout that, Doctor Toppman. I'm always forgetting that you folks like bein' called that.

TOPPMAN. I'm really very busy right now. Can it wait?

AARON. Well, I …

TOPPMAN. Good. Now, if you don't mind …

AARON. Yes, sir, Mister … I mean, Doctor Toppman. I guess I'll go to the other offices …

TOPPMAN. *(Reading)* Fine. Fine. *(AARON starts to leave but looks back at TOPPMAN before exiting. TOPPMAN takes the brandy out of the drawer and pours himself another drink. As he puts down the snifter, something catches his eye. He stares at the obelisk and then reaches for it. As he touches it he notices a small, chipped section. He is puzzled and when he picks it up, it breaks in two, the larger piece in his hand and the base remaining on top of the desk.)* What the … *(He places the larger piece back onto the base. It fits together well, missing only the small chip. He picks it up again, puts it back together and then begins looking around. He first searches the desktop and then moves to the office floor. He sees something under one of the office chairs and gets on his hands and knees to have a closer look. He picks the object up, brings it over to his desk and places it on the obelisk, where it fits perfectly. He sits down behind his desk and pours another drink, all the while staring at the obelisk. He finishes the drink, puts the brandy and the snifter away, turns off the music and crosses to the door. Opening door.)* Aaron!

AARON. *(Offstage)* Yes, sir, Mis … Doctor Toppman?

TOPPMAN. I'd like to see you in my office, please.

AARON. *(Offstage)* Be right there. *(TOPPMAN returns to his desk and sits down. A few moments later, AARON enters.)* Yes, Doctor Toppman?

TOPPMAN. What did you want to talk to me about?

AARON. Oh, it wasn't nothin' important.

TOPPMAN. It seemed fairly urgent before.

AARON. No, it wasn't nothin'.

TOPPMAN. You're sure?

AARON. Yes, sir.

TOPPMAN. Okay. I just thought I'd check.

AARON. I appreciate it, Doctor Toppman. Good night.

TOPPMAN. Good night, Aaron. *(AARON heads for the door.)* Oh, Aaron …

AARON. *(Turning)* Yes, Doctor Toppman?

TOPPMAN. You wouldn't happen to know how this … *(He stands and lifts the top of the broken obelisk off its base.)* … happened, would you?

AARON. *(Looking at it.)* Uhh …

TOPPMAN. I don't seem to remember it being broken when I left this afternoon.

AARON… No, sir. At least not last night.

TOPPMAN. At least not what last night?

AARON. It wasn't broke last night.

TOPPMAN. No, I don't think it was. In fact, I don't think it was broken when I left my office this afternoon.

AARON. I wouldn't know nothin' 'bou that. I didn't get here 'til five-fifteen.

TOPPMAN. I see. So you know nothing about this?

(He places the top obelisk on his desk.)

AARON. *(Flatly)* I didn't break it.
TOPPMAN. *(Sitting down.)* There's no point in lying, Aaron.
AARON. I said I didn't break it.
TOPPMAN. Not on purpose, perhaps.
AARON. Not at all.

(He turns to leave and TOPPMAN jumps up.)

TOPPMAN. Where do you think you're going?
AARON. *(Turning around.)* Back to work. I've got a lot of offices to clean.
TOPPMAN. *(Picking up obelisk.)* This was a very expensive gift.
AARON. Yeah. I'm sure it was.
TOPPMAN. You're sure you don't have anything to tell me?
AARON. I'm not one of your students, Doctor Toppman.
TOPPMAN. What is that supposed to mean?
AARON. It means you could treat me with a little respect.
TOPPMAN. Oh, it's respect you want, huh? *(He comes out from behind the desk and approaches AARON, who stands his ground.)* I find it hard to respect someone who lies to me. Don't you?
AARON. I said I didn't break your damn statue.
TOPPMAN. *(Smirking)* It's … it was, an obelisk. Not a "so-called" statue.
AARON. Whatever. *(AARON again turns to the door and is about to exit when TOPPMAN goes to his phone and starts dialing. AARON turning around.)* Who you callin'?
TOPPMAN. *(While dialing.)* You'll find out.
AARON. I asked who you're callin'?
TOPPMAN. Officer Jenkins? Yes, this is Doctor Toppman …

(Looking at AARON.)

AARON. Don't this beat all.
TOPPMAN. *(Into phone.)* Could you hold on for a second? Someone just came into my office. *(Putting his hand over the receiver and addressing AARON.)* You were saying?
AARON. Them kids is right.
TOPPMAN. Are right. What are they right about?

(AARON stares at TOPPMAN and hesitates before answering.)

AARON. You is an asshole.

(TOPPMAN, furious, takes his hand off the receiver.)

TOPPMAN. *(Into phone.)* Officer Jenkins? Let me call you right back. *(Hanging up.)* How dare you say that to me! Do you know who I am?

AARON. Yeah. I know all about you, Doc-tor Toppman.

TOPPMAN. Maybe you and I and your supervisor need to sit down and discuss your work habits.

AARON. My work habits is fine.

TOPPMAN. And your grammar is atrocious.

AARON. *(Frowning)* That supposed to be some kind of insult?

TOPPMAN. *(Wryly)* Insult. Compliment. Who knows?

AARON. You really think you're somethin', don't you?

TOPPMAN. What I think is irrelevant to the matter at hand.

AARON. There ain't no "matter at hand" here.

TOPPMAN. One, there's the broken obelisk. Two, there's your refusal to accept responsibility for ...

AARON. What do you know about responsibility?

TOPPMAN. I think I know quite ...

AARON. Man, you don't know nothin'.

TOPPMAN. Is that so? Pray tell.

AARON. What?

TOPPMAN. Tell me what I don't know about responsibility.

AARON. You don't wanna hear what I gots to say.

TOPPMAN. *(Sitting down on the corner of his desk.)* No, really. I'm sure I'll find it very edifying.

AARON. Eda-what?

TOPPMAN. It means ...

AARON. Man, who you think you are, God? You sittin' there callin' me a liar and then callin' the campus police real sly like ...

TOPPMAN. Is there a point to this?

AARON. Yeah, there's a point ... *(Pointing at TOPPMAN.)* You think you real smart, don't you? You gonna call the police and tell them that someone broke your statue ...

TOPPMAN. Obelisk ...

AARON. Whatever. Then you tell them you think I done it, right?

TOPPMAN. *(Smirking)* Please. Continue. I find this fascinating.

AARON. *(More defiantly.)* Then they ask me and I says no. Then you tell Mr. William what you think I done and he fires me. That about how you got it planned?

TOPPMAN. *(Smiling)* Not how I would have said it, but you've got the general idea.

AARON. So you gonna get me fired 'cause I won't say I broke your...

TOPPMAN. Obelisk ...

AARON. ... when I didn't ...

TOPPMAN. That's what you say.

AARON. Man, why don't you just call me "nigger."

TOPPMAN. This has nothing to do with race!

AARON. That's what all you say. "Oh, it don't have nothin' to do with your race, Aaron." I heard that all my life. I think I liked it better when people's called you nigger to your face instead a behind your back.

TOPPMAN. *(Standing up.)* I have never called ...

AARON. Oh, no. Not you. You never called no one nigger, has you?

TOPPMAN. I ...

AARON. You one a them nice white folk who thinks we black folk been culturally deprived. Thinks we deserve every opportunity to be just like you and all your white friends.

TOPPMAN. Now look here, I went to public schools and ...

AARON. ... some of your best friends is black, huh?

TOPPMAN. I don't have to listen to ...

AARON. Yes, you do. You found it ... fascinatin' ... thems your words, ain't they?

TOPPMAN. That was ...

AARON. ... before I made you uncomfortable by saying "nigger?"

TOPPMAN. Don't use that word ...

AARON. *(Moving closer.)* Nigger. *(Takes another step.)* NIGGER. *(In TOPPMAN's face.)* NIGGER! *(Laughing)* You don't like hearin' it, do you?

TOPPMAN. *(Shaking head.)* I don't ...

AARON. Well, I heard it alls my life. And if anybody's gonna say it, it's me.

TOPPMAN. Your race is irrelevant ... *(Backing behind desk.)* ... it wouldn't matter if you were black or white or red or ...

AARON. Purple? Man, you ever seen any purple people? I never have and I been around a lot longer than you. Why white folks try to cover up their prejudice with some silly-ass statement like that? Huh?

TOPPMAN. What I meant was ...

AARON. I knowed what you mean.

TOPPMAN. I don't think you understand ...

AARON. Just because you got your P, H and D, doesn't mean I don't know what you're sayin'.

TOPPMAN. What I'm saying is that your being African-American has nothing to do with my accusing you of breaking the obelisk. You're the one with the master key ...

AARON. A whole bunch a people got master keys ...

TOPPMAN. But you're the only one that comes in here, in my office, every day.

AARON. So if somebody else ... a white janitor, cleaned your office every day, you'd be blamin' him?

TOPPMAN. Exactly.. That's what I'm ...

AARON. Bull-shit!

TOPPMAN. There's no need to resort to profanity.

AARON. It ain't profanity when it's the truth.

TOPPMAN. Truth! What do you know about the truth?

AARON. You wanna know the truth? I'll tell you the truth. You go on and tell them that I broke that oba-whatever, and they'll fire me. That's the truth! Then how's my kids supposed to eat? How's they supposed to go to school and become somethin'?

TOPPMAN. No one said anything about firing you ...

AARON. And no one will 'til they do it. That's the truth! But you, you don't got nothin' to be worried about ...

TOPPMAN. I assure you, I face the same day to day difficulties that...

AARON. "Day to day difficulties ..." That's a joke. What you got to be worried about? You got tenure. That's a white man's welfare. You gotta stay alive and you makes your money. Me. Me, I gotta work two jobs justa stay outta jail.

TOPPMAN. I didn't know ...

AARON. There's a lot you don't know, mister Top-man. And the thing is, you never stops to think about anyone else neither. How long I been cleanin' your office?

TOPPMAN. I'm not sure. I ...

AARON. Seven years. Seven years I been cleanin' your office and the first time in all those years you say somethin' to me, you callin' me a liar.

TOPPMAN. I did not call you a ...

AARON. But you meant it, didn't you?

TOPPMAN. I ...

AARON. You don't need to answer. I already knows what you're gonna say. The whole things almost kinda funny.

TOPPMAN. Funny how?

AARON. If I'd a been smart enough, it'd be you gonna be fired instead a me.

TOPPMAN. Why would I be fired?

AARON. Ain't no use a getting' into it now. No one's gonna believe me. Still, I had the chance.

TOPPMAN. What could you possibly say that would get me fired?

AARON. Plenty a things.

TOPPMAN. Name one.

AARON. Drinkin' on the job.

TOPPMAN. That's preposterous.

AARON. Don't matter what kinda fancy words you throw out, facts is facts.

TOPPMAN. I never, ever come to the college drunk.

AARON. No one ever said you did, mister Top-man. I just said you drinks on the job.

TOPPMAN. Perhaps a little taste now and then.

AARON. *(Laughing)* A little taste, huh?

TOPPMAN. That's right. At most.

AARON. More like a pint a month of them good ol' Christian Brothers.

TOPPMAN. I never ...

AARON. 'fact, I'd be willin' to bet that there's a bottle in the middle left drawer right now.

TOPPMAN. That's patently ridiculous. Like everyone else, I have an occasional drink. I haven't done anything wrong.

AARON. What about that blonde?

TOPPMAN. What blonde?

AARON. That one in your night class last semester.

TOPPMAN. I don't know what you're talking about.

AARON. Oh, you know, mister Top-man. You and that blonde ... in this office ... late at night ...

TOPPMAN. I have no idea ...

AARON. Don't try to bull me, mister. I may be dumb but I isn't stupid.

TOPPMAN. I think maybe you ...

AARON. Ain't no maybes about it. I know what I seen. Only maybe I knows is maybe I tell or maybe I won't.

TOPPMAN. That's blackmail!

AARON. There you go again, makin' race an issue.

TOPPMAN. By blackmail I mean ...

AARON. I know what you mean. Sometimes you P, H, and D doctors is about the stupidest people I know. *(Serious.)* I ain't plannin' on blackmailin' no one. Not even you, mister doctor Toppman. *(A beat.)* No, there ain't no reason for me to make no waves.

TOPPMAN. I see. I'm supposed to forget about my broken obelisk and then there won't be any reason for you to report me. Is that it?

AARON. First, I got nothin' to do with your broken oba-lisk. And second, I ain't got no plans to file no report. I's just lettin' you know that I know what you do.

TOPPMAN. How long have you been spying on me?

AARON. I ain't been doin' no spyin'.

TOPPMAN. What would you call it?

AARON. I just noticed things, that's all.

TOPPMAN. And I suppose it's merely a coincidence that you're making these observations public at the same time I'm accusing you of breaking my obelisk?

AARON. One don't have nothin' to do with the other.

TOPPMAN. Maybe I should call Officer Jenkins?

AARON. Maybe you should.

TOPPMAN. *(Crossing to phone.)* I think I will. Then you can tell your story and I'll tell mine and we'll see who they believe.

AARON. I suspect they'll believe you.

TOPPMAN. Damn right they will.

AARON. Until they find that pint of Christian Brothers in your drawer.

(TOPPMAN opens the drawer, takes out the bottle of brandy and crosses to the door. He opens the door and tosses the bottle into AARON's trash can. He lets the door close as he marches back to the desk.)

TOPPMAN. So much for your evidence.

AARON. Yes sir, you sure did get rid of that brandy.

TOPPMAN. That's right, I did.

AARON. But you didn't do nothin' about the evidence I got.

TOPPMAN. *(Smile fading.)* What evidence?

AARON. Oh, don't you worry none about it.

TOPPMAN. You're bluffing.

AARON. Maybe I is and maybe I ain't.

TOPPMAN. You don't have any evidence. What evidence could you have?

AARON. Nothin' much. *(A beat.)* Maybe a picture or two.

TOPPMAN. A picture of what?

AARON. Of who?

TOPPMAN. A picture of who?

AARON. It was a real stormy, rainy night. Ligtnin' flashin' all over the place. One little flashbulb wasn't gonna make a difference now was it, doctor Top-man?

TOPPMAN. You're lying.

AARON. Well, maybe I is and maybe I isn't.

TOPPMAN. You don't have any photographs. You can't bluff me. *(Picks up phone and starts dialing.)* We'll see what evidence you have. *(Into phone.)* Officer Jenkins? This is Doctor Toppman again. Sorry about the confusion earlier. A problem? Yes, you could say I have a problem. It seems somebody ... *(Raising eyebrows and staring at AARON.)* ... entered my office and destroyed a very valuable possession. Yes, I do have a certain suspicion about who might have done it. No, no. I understand. I'll be in my office for the next hour or so. Whenever you can get to it. Thank you, Officer Jenkins. *(Hangs up the phone and smiles at AARON.)* Now we'll see who has what.

AARON. *(Smiling)* You is about as stupid as they say you is.

TOPPMAN. *(Tersely)* I won't stand for these insults.

AARON. *(Laughing and shuffling his feet like a boxer.)* What you gonna do? Knock me out?

TOPPMAN. There's no reason to make this any more unpleasant than it already is. You can finish your rounds, I'll wait for Officer Jenkins.

AARON. You do that, mister doctor Toppman.

(AARON crosses to the door and exits. TOPPMAN goes to the door and locks it from the inside. He goes back to his desk, picks up the phone

*and dials. He picks up the top of the obelisk as he waits for an
answer.)*

TOPPMAN. *(Into phone.)* Carolyn? I'm still at work. No, I'm going
to be a little late tonight. Oh, I've got a few things to take care of at
school. I know that I was late last night, honey. I just can't help it, I'm
waiting in my office for someone. He should be here in the next hour or ...
*(AARON reappears, in the door window. He knocks on the door to attract
TOPPMAN's attention.)* Hold on, Carolyn, somebody's at the door.
(TOPPMAN puts phone down and crosses to the door. To AARON.) What
do you want?

(AARON puts his face to the window.)

AARON. I got somethin' to show you.
TOPPMAN. I'm on the phone. *(TOPPMAN turns and walks back to
the desk. As he picks up the phone, AARON uses his key and opens the
door. Into phone.)* It was no ... *(TOPPMAN hears AARON entering the
office. To AARON.)* I thought I told you that I was ... *(AARON has crossed
to TOPPMAN and throws a photograph down on the desk. Into phone.)*
It's okay, honey, it's just ... *(Sees photograph.)* Where the Hell did ...
(Into phone.) No, Carolyn. I'm fine, really. *(Glaring at AARON while
speaking into the phone.)* No, it wasn't who I expected. I'll call you when
I'm ready to leave. Yes, I love you, too.

(TOPPMAN hangs up the phone and picks up the photograph.)

AARON. Right good picture, don't you think?
TOPPMAN. Where did you get this?
AARON. I already done told you when I took the picture.
TOPPMAN. How dare you invade my privacy!
AARON. Looks like you're the one that's invading privates.
TOPPMAN. *(Tears picture into several pieces.)* What I do in my
office is my business. Mine and mine alone. Do you understand me?
AARON. Better than you know, mister Top-man. *(Whispering)* By the
way, I got plenty of those pictures.
TOPPMAN. *(Red-faced)* And what do you plan on doing with them?
AARON. I ain't got no plans for them.
TOPPMAN. You're not planning to show them to anybody? Say my
wife or the Dean?
AARON. Not unless there's some reason to.
TOPPMAN. Like filing a report on this broken obelisk?
AARON. You go ahead and file your report ...
TOPPMAN. But?
AARON. Ain't no need in blamin' it on me since I didn't do it.

(TOPPMAN picks up the broken obelisk and points it in AARON's face.)

TOPPMAN. You don't have anything to worry about if you're telling the truth.

AARON. Sometimes the truth ain't enough for the black man.

TOPPMAN. What do you mean, the truth isn't enough?

AARON. Sometimes people finds out about a fella's past and they don't care about the truth.

TOPPMAN. Something in your past?

AARON. Uh huh. Now I don't par-tic-ular-ly want to see you get in trouble. But the way I see it, better you than me.

TOPPMAN. What is it that you did?

AARON. You don't wanna know.

TOPPMAN. I'm dying to know. *(TOPPMAN puts down the obelisk and comes around the desk to where AARON stands. Smiling.)* What is it? Flunk out of high school? Get arrested for being drunk? Had to get married?

(AARON is getting more and more impatient as TOPPMAN runs through the questions. When he asks the last one, AARON lunges forward, grabs TOPPMAN by the neck and slams him down onto the desk. His hands around TOPPMAN's neck, AARON thrusts his face to within an inch of the professor's.)

AARON. I killed a man!

(AARON lets go of TOPPMAN and crosses to the professor's bookshelf, as he tries to collect himself. TOPPMAN, gasping for air, slowly pulls himself off the desk and stands with hiss hands on his knees as he recovers.)

TOPPMAN. You … you're crazy … you tried to … to kill me …

(AARON turns around and stares at TOPPMAN.)

AARON. If I wanted to kill you, you'd be dead.

TOPPMAN. You can't get …

AARON. Get away with it? No, maybe not. But nobody … not you, not nobody says somethin' dirty about my wife. Not and stay standin', they don't.

TOPPMAN. I didn't mean any …

AARON. Disrespect? Man, all you given me this evenin' is disrespect. You blame me for somethin' I didn't do … you call my wife dirty … *(Tears in his eyes.)* You call that respect? You don't know nothin' about me. You don't know nothin' about my life. You don't know what a sweet smile that woman a mine had … what a pure heart and a sweet smile she …

TOPPMAN. Had?

AARON. *(Rubbing at his eyes.)* She passed on three years back ...

TOPPMAN. I'm sorry, I didn't ...

AARON. Know? No, why shoulda you known? What do you care about a janitor.

TOPPMAN. I didn't know. I guess I should have asked.

AARON. That's right, you should've done a lotta things since you been here. And there's a lotta things you did, you shouldn't a done. I'm a person, too. I likes to be said hello to and asked how's I doin'. Everyone does.

TOPPMAN. I didn't think ...

AARON. That's the problem with some a you professors. You so smart that sometimes you don't think much.

TOPPMAN. I guess not.

AARON. You guess right. Like that girl in your class. You ever stop to think who you'd be hurtin' by carryin' on with her like you did?

TOPPMAN. I wasn't hurting any ...

AARON. What about your wife? Carolyn's her name, ain't it?

TOPPMAN. That's right. How'd you ...

AARON. I heard you talkin' to her tonight.

TOPPMAN. And you remembered her name?

AARON. Yeah. What you think she'd feel, if it woulda been her up here that night findin' you and that blonde on the floor?

TOPPMAN. She never ... That's not the point, is it?

AARON. No, it ain't. I don't know what kinda woman your wife is, mister Toppman. But if she's any kinda wife at all ...

TOPPMAN. She's a good wife ... a good woman.

AARON. Then why you getting' mixed up with that girl?

TOPPMAN. It's complicated.

AARON. Too complicated for someone like me to understand?

TOPPMAN. I didn't mean it that way. Our marriage wasn't in good shape at the time ...

AARON. And you slippin' it to that coed was gonna help it?

TOPPMAN. She was interested in me. Attracted to me. She made me feel good.

AARON. You feel good about you and her now?

TOPPMAN. No.

AARON. I didn't think so. Let me tell you somethin', mister Toppman. My daddy had a sayin', "da grass always looks greener on da other side of the fence but jumpin over da fence ain't gonna do nothin' for your own lawn." *(Smiles)* I can remember when things weren't so good 'tween me and Olivia. She caught me flirtin' with some other gal and she almost tore my head off my shoulders. *(AARON laughs. TOPPMAN looks at him and chuckles with him.)* That woman, she'd go wild when she got mad ...

(He pauses, deep in thought.)

TOPPMAN. How did she ...

(He can't finish the sentence. AARON looks at him.)

AARON. Die? *(TOPPMAN nods. AARON puts his hand to his mouth and pauses momentarily.)* Cancer. *(A beat.)* Cancer cut down one Hell of a woman.
TOPPMAN. I'm sorry.
AARON. *(Nodding in acknowledgment.)* Yes, sir. My Olivia was one damn fine woman. Fought it all the way. She never once thought she was licked. I knew. I knew it was only a matter of time before she was gonna be taken away. But she never gave up. Not even when she was layin' on her death bed. *(Pauses)* Told me she was tired. Said, "I'm gonna take a little nap, Aaron. Don't you let me sleep too long." That was it. Her eyes closed and then she slipped off for good.

(TOPPMAN crosses to AARON and puts his hand on the older man's shoulder.)

TOPPMAN. I don't know what to say.
AARON. Ain't nothin' to say.
TOPPMAN. How long had the two of you been married?
AARON. *(His face lighting up.)* Twenty-nine years. Got hitched in July 1958.
TOPPMAN. Fifty-eight? I was four years old.
AARON. *(Laughing)* I bet you was a pain in the butt even back then.
TOPPMAN. I was never ... *(Smiles)* Yes, I guess I was.
AARON. Damn right you was. *(Pauses)* How long you and the missus been together?
TOPPMAN. Eight ... no, seven years this December. We, uh ...
AARON. You love her?
TOPPMAN. Of course ...
AARON. Then why you doin' her wrong?
TOPPMAN. I'm not ...
AARON. Adultery helpin' your marriage, is it?
TOPPMAN. It was one time ... one person ...
AARON. One time too many.
TOPPMAN. Not all marriages are wonderful all the time, Aaron.
AARON. And cheatin' make it wonderful?
TOPPMAN. No. But people grow apart. Like in "Virginia Woolf."
AARON. Who?
TOPPMAN. "Who's Afraid of Virginia Woolf?", the play. George and Martha.
AARON. Never heard of it.
TOPPMAN. You've never seen the play?
AARON. Nope.

TOPPMAN. What about the movie? Elizabeth Taylor and Richard Burton.

AARON. When it out?

TOPPMAN. I don't know. Let me see. *(TOPPMAN walks to his bookshelf, runs his hand along the middle shelf and comes across the play. He opens it and crosses back to AARON.)* The play was produced in nineteen sixty-two and the movie in nineteen sixty-four.

AARON. Didn't see too many movies back then.

TOPPMAN. No time?

AARON. No, sir. Had plenty a time.

TOPPMAN. Too expensive?

AARON. Yes, sir. But that ain't the reason.

TOPPMAN. So?

AARON. I's in prison in nineteen and sixty-four.

TOPPMAN. Oh. *(A beat.)* For killing a man?

AARON. That's right.

TOPPMAN. *(Handing play to AARON.)* Well, here. You can read my copy. It's a fascinating play.

AARON. I don't think so.

(AARON hands the play back to TOPPMAN.)

TOPPMAN. No, really. I don't mind. Keep it.

AARON. I don't read.

TOPPMAN. No time, huh?

AARON. Can't read.

TOPPMAN. You can't ...

AARON. Words is just a jumbled up buncha letters to me.

TOPPMAN. Oh.

AARON. I makes due.

TOPPMAN. I'm sure you do. *(A beat.)* Didn't you go to school?

AARON. Through the first half a fifth grade. Then my papa died and I had to go to work.

TOPPMAN. When you were eleven?

AARON. Uh huh. Nineteen and forty-six. Worked in the fields for thirty cents an hour. Them was good times. Hard work but good times.

TOPPMAN. But you raised a family ...

AARON. Two boys and a girl. Me and Olivia lost two babies but the other ones are doin' fine.

TOPPMAN. How did you do it? Without an education ... without being able to read?

AARON. I worked hard. I learned enough to get by on. Got me a job with city sanitation in nineteen and sixty-five and worked a whole lotta different night jobs until the college hired me fourteen years ago.

TOPPMAN. That's what you do during the day?

AARON. That's right. I pick up people's trash during the day and at night. I pick up your trash.

TOPPMAN. You know where I live?

AARON. You live in that brick bungalow on East Sycamore. The one with a swing on the porch. Been pickin' up at your place on Tuesday's since you moved to town. Picked up the Weidman's garbage before they sold the place to you.

TOPPMAN. I've never seen you.

AARON. You don't look. I see you plenty. Pullin' outta the driveway … shovelin' the walk … *(A beat.)* How come you never leave nothin' for the Holidays?

TOPPMAN. Leave?

AARON. A gift. Everybody else on East Sycamore leave us a present for the Holidays.

TOPPMAN. I never thought about it.

AARON. Like I said before, Doctor Toppman. People like other people's to notice them.

TOPPMAN. I'm sorry. I didn't realize.

AARON. I wouldn't worry about it. There's mostly too much cookies and beer anyway.

TOPPMAN. Why'd you do it, Aaron?

AARON. Do what?

TOPPMAN. Kill a man.

AARON. I don't talk about it much.

TOPPMAN. I realize that. You don't seem like somebody who would…

AARON. Kill somebody?

TOPPMAN. Uh huh.

AARON. I can't say I regret doin' it.

TOPPMAN. Even though you went to prison?

AARON. The man had it comin' to him for what he did. *(Seeing that TOPPMAN is sincerely interested.)* The man I killed raped and murdered my baby. *(TOPPMAN gasps.)* And they let him off on a tech … techni …

TOPPMAN. Technicality?

AARON. That's it. Said they had violated his rights. What about my baby's rights? What about a parent's right to see their baby grow up?

TOPPMAN. So you killed him?

AARON. I hunted him down. You know what he did when I found him? *(TOPPMAN shakes his head.)* He laughed in my face! Called me a fool! That's when I did it. I pulled the gun out and shot him dead. Then I laughed in his face… Called him a fool. Then the police came. They didn't make no technicality with me, no sir. Sentenced me to ten years.

TOPPMAN. You were in prison for ten years?

AARON. Six years, seven months, one week, two days. Got out early for good behavior.

TOPPMAN. What about your lawyer? Did he appeal?

AARON. Ain't no appeals for a black man in nineteen and sixty-one. Never seen the lawyer before or since.

TOPPMAN. Jesus Christ!

AARON. Now Him I seen.

TOPPMAN. What?

AARON. Found Him in prison. Never had time for no religion 'til then. Now I know the way.

TOPPMAN. It's unfair. You never should have been convicted of murder.

AARON. Life's unfair, Doctor Toppman. Sooner I learnt that, the better off I was. *(Looking at clock on TOPPMAN's desk.)* Look at that. Seven-fifteen already. I better get to them other offices.

TOPPMAN. Wait. *(Picks up phone and dials.)* Officer Jenkins? No, no. I found out what happened to my obelisk. An obelisk. It was an accident. You don't need to come by. Thank you, officer.

(Hangs up.)

AARON. You didn't need to do that.

TOPPMAN. Yes, I did. It's about time I stopped blaming others for what happens to me.

AARON. Now that's a start. You know what you need to do next?

TOPPMAN. I think so.

AARON. What?

TOPPMAN. I need to go home to my wife.

AARON. That's right. You do that. Ain't nothin' more important than the love of a good woman.

TOPPMAN. Carolyn's a good woman.

AARON. You ain't so bad yourself.

TOPPMAN. Thank you, Aaron.

AARON. For what?

TOPPMAN. For tonight. I got one Hell of an education this evening.

AARON. Ain't that a kick in the pants.

TOPPMAN. It certainly was.

AARON. Goodnight, Doctor Toppman.

(Turns to exit.)

TOPPMAN. Please, call me Stephen.

AARON. *(Turning back, smiling.)* Goodnight, Stephen.

(AARON exits. TOPPMAN looks around the office, takes a deep breath and then picks up the phone and dials.)

TOPPMAN. Hi, honey. We can't go out tonight. No, it's my wife. I need to spend more time with her. People are ge ng suspicious, Nancy. I'll see you soon. I promise. I love you, too.

(He puts down the phone and picks up his briefcase. Crossing to the door, he turns off the lights and then exits. His silhouette can be seen through the window as he locks the door and walks down the hall.)

(Several moments later, we see AARON's silhouette in the door window. He unlocks the door and enters the office, turning on the lights as the door closes behind him. He crosses to TOPPMAN's desk and picks up the play. He sits down in TOPPMAN's chair and begins reading as the lights fade to blackout.)

END OF PLAY

COSTUME PLOT

TOPPMAN:
Tweed jacket, khaki chino pants, yellow shirt, green & navy tie, brown shoes & belt

AARON:
Gray coveralls, work boots, old beat-up baseball cap

PROPERTY PLOT

9' x 12' Area rug
Wooden teacher's desk
Office Chair
Wastebasket
Bookcases
Sofa
A wooden office door with pebbled glass window, set into a door frame. Should swing into the space and towards downstage. This door and frame are attached to a partial wall going upstage and downstage to provide a feeling of separation between the office area and the "hallway" outside the door.
Books & set dressing on bookshelves, including copy of "Who's Afraid of Virginia Woolf"
Desk items, including tape, stapler, in baskets, desk blotter, phone, etc.
Gray marble obelisk, broken into two parts and set up to appear unbroken
Briefcase for Toppman
Files and papers in briefcase
Small executive CD player on desk
CD of Mozart's requiem in desk
Brandy snifter
Pint bottle of Christian Brothers brandy
Wheeled janitor's cart with mop/brooms, etc.
Photographs of Toppman and girl
Desk lamp
Desk clock

EVENING EDUCATION

SET DRAWING

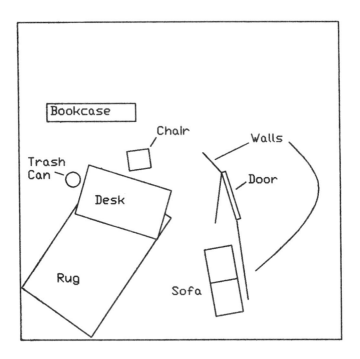

HOT ROD

by
Jeremy Kareken

Thanks to
Brandy Hotchner, Gene Lasko and Deborah Medwin.
Extra special thanks to an extra special registration partner:
Gail Griffin.

HOT ROD was originally performed at a workshop production at the Love Creek Off-Off-Broadway Festival. It was directed by Joe Ametrano with the following cast:

JEN . . . . Meghan McGrath

MARCUS . . . . Vito Puliafito

JULIE . . . . Brandy Hotchner

ABOUT THE AUTHOR

JEREMY KAREKEN was born in Rochester, New York and attended the University of Chicago, where he got his start acting, writing and directing with the comedy troupe *Off-Off-Campus*. He received his MFA from the Actors Studio Drama School at New School University. His play *Big Train* was performed in Melbourne, Australia, New York City and at the Actors Theatre of Louisville. *Duck, Rabbit, Duck* was produced at the Andrews Lane in Dublin, Ireland. He also wrote *The Bradleys,* the stage adaptation of the works of comic-book artist and author Peter Bagge.

CHARACTERS

> JULIE: A bridal registrar
> JEN: A bride
> MARCUS: Her fiancé

SETTING

> Place: Bridal registry office at a major department store
> Time: Now

(At rise: JEN and MARCUS, two affianced lovers, are mooning at each other in an upscale department store. MARCUS is dressed well, but he's a joe-six-pack sort, who doesn't feel comfortable being dressed well. JEN is professionally and stylishly dressed. Everything about her is perfect. Enter JULIE. JULIE, unlike JEN, is a complete mess. Although she's wearing similar clothes to JEN, the clothes just look wrong. Her hair's a wreck and she snorts throughout the scene, as though getting over post-nasal drip. As the scene progresses, the snorting becomes more compulsive. JEN and MARCUS' legs are visible to the audience.)

JULIE. Sorry to keep you waiting, I had to take that call. I don't know why he bugs me at work.
MARCUS. No, that's fine.
JULIE. You know how it is.
JEN. We sure do.
JULIE. *Snort.*
MARCUS. Hmm?
JULIE. What?
MARCUS. Oh, I thought you said something.

(JEN kicks MARCUS. Slightly.)

JULIE. No, no. Wow. Look at you.
JEN. Yeah.
JULIE. Look at you.
JEN. Yeah.
JULIE. You getting excited?
JEN. We sure are.
JULIE. Well it's an exciting time. Where are you getting married?
JEN. Upstate.
JULIE. Oh, that's nice. Nice country wedding?
JEN. Yes.

(Pause. JULIE gives JEN the once over and looks at MARCUS.)

JULIE. I hope you planned a honeymoon, young man.
MARCUS. On it. I'm right there.
JULIE. Good, because I didn't get to go on one and it ruined my whole marriage.
MARCUS. Well I'm on it.

JULIE. Okay. Well. Great. Let's get started. *(Pause. Pause. Explode.)* Have you ever been married before?!

MARCUS & JEN. No, no. First time.

(Pause)

JULIE. Really? First time, huh? Because you look —

JEN. We wanted to be sure.

JULIE. Huh.

(Pause)

MARCUS. First time.

JULIE. I have to ask that. Because there's different gifts. People need different things for their second marriage. Plus, family and friends don't want to pony up for gifts for a second marriage. So we have a second catalogue for that. It's a cheaper catalogue. I don't know why people even bother with a second marriage, you know. They should just go down to city hall or shack up or go to Vegas and stop bothering me, you know? *Snort.*

MARCUS. Yeah, well … this is our first.

JEN. That won't happen to us.

JULIE. You're fighting against statistics.

MARCUS. Really?

JULIE. 54% of marriages end in divorce.

MARCUS. We'll try to keep that in mind.

JEN. I like to think of it as 46% of marriages end in —

JULIE. Death? *Snort.*

MARCUS. Happy ever after.

(JULIE snorts. Pause.)

JULIE. Gohd, listen to me, you're about to have the happiest occasion of your life and I'm talking about divorce; is that stupid or what?

JEN. Well, I guess you do have to be realistic these days.

JULIE. It's true. If I ever get stuck in a relationship again, I'm going in with my eyes open.

JEN. Me too.

MARCUS. What?

JEN. Just kidding, Honey Bear.

JULIE. Honey Bear?

MARCUS. Oh, do NOT call me that in public. NOT a public name.

JULIE. I think it's sweet. Look! He's blushing.

MARCUS. Oh, knock it off you two.

JEN. Sorry. *(Pause)* HONEY BEAR!

MARCUS. Fine, you've all had your laugh. Can we get on with it?

(JULIE snorts. Pause.)

JULIE. Okay. Let's do this. It's really pretty simple. All you have to do is look through the catalogue, and enter the product numbers here. Then the quantity over here in this column here.

MARCUS. Great. Now which are the product numbers?

(JULIE slams her hand down onto the catalogue.)

JULIE. These! With the three digits! And then the letter! And then the four digits!

MARCUS. Oh, I see.

(JULIE snorts.)

JEN. Let me see the catalogue.

MARCUS. Come on, I get it first.

JULIE. Boys.

JEN. I know.

JULIE. I have two catalogues for this very purpose.

JEN. Thank God.

(JULIE looks in her desk for a couple of seconds.)

JULIE. Huh.

JEN. What?

JULIE. I don't seem to have one.

MARCUS. *(Not relinquishing the catalogue.)* That's okay, we can share.

JEN. You see his idea of sharing?

MARCUS. Oh, knock it off —

JEN. Honey Bear!

MARCUS. Sweetie Boo! Oooh! Look at this! The JuiceMaster 9000!

JEN. What the hell is that?

MARCUS. It juices on a timer. You put the fruits and the vegetables in the night before and the next morning, you have a pitcher of juice.

JEN. We don't need that.

MARCUS. But it juices. On a timer.

JEN. We don't need that. Look at the china patterns.

MARCUS. I don't need any plates.

JEN. We need plates.

MARCUS. The Cuisinart Grind 'n' Brew. Look at this! It grinds and it brews. First it grinds, then it brews.

JEN. Hence the name. Come on. Let me look at it.

MARCUS. Give me a minute. Oooh …

JULIE. I just broke up with my boyfriend.
MARCUS. Maybe he took the other catalogue.

(JEN kicks MARCUS, under the table.)

JULIE. *Snort.* Well, husband. Well, both. I didn't know what he was. He should have been a boyfriend, but he got too close. I hate it when they get too close.
JEN. Yeah. I mean, I ... don't —
JULIE. Except when they're obviously as happy as you two. I can tell all about happy couples. I see a million of them every year. At least it feels like it. Day after day. Anyways, there you are, and you really seem like a together couple to me.
JEN. Yeah?
JULIE. Yeah. Not like us.
JEN. Well, I'm sorry.
MARCUS. You should have let him have the catalogue.

(Kick)

JULIE. My husband ... he was a pig.
JEN. I know the feeling.
MARCUS. *Oink.*
JULIE. *Snort.*
JEN. Come on, give me the catalogue.
MARCUS. In a minute.
JULIE. He didn't understand my boundaries. You know how it is.
JEN. Completely. You have to let him know what's yours and what's his.
JULIE. It's so true. The more I talked it over with my friends, I knew that it was all a boundary issue. He kept invading me. Getting in my space. Not that you two have a problem with that. Of course it seems like you two have a healthy relationship. *Snort.*
JEN. I like to think we do. C'mon, let me see the —
MARCUS. Where are the espresso mach — oh, never mind, I see them.
JULIE. I think it's all about developing a safe space. It's one of the principles I live by. Do you know what I mean?
JEN. Sure. Sure. Boundaries are very important; the other day I found a beard hair on my toothbrush.
JULIE. ICK! Ew.
JEN. Isn't that gross?
MARCUS. Immersion blenders ...
JEN. I couldn't believe it. I thought I'd kill him.
JULIE. I would have killed him. You have a lot of tolerance.
JEN. Tell me about it. Just look at him.

MARCUS. Oh, very nice.

JULIE. *Snort.* I know. Well, it's nice you're getting married. You look very happy together. Not like myself and — Rod.

JEN. You were dating a guy named Rod?

JULIE. No, that's just what I called him. *(MARCUS looks up. Before he can say anything, JEN kicks him. JULIE snorts.)* So what's the secret? How do you stay together?

MARCUS. Fuck if I know.

JEN. Marcus!

MARCUS. Sorry. Pardon my French and all.

JULIE. Well, I just think it's important to keep up the boundaries.

MARCUS. What is this with the boundaries? Huh?

JULIE. It's important.

MARCUS. You think that's important? With men it's always about communication and letting the guard down so you can talk about things, but with women it's about building these walls, I just never get it.

(JEN kicks MARCUS. She misses and hits JULIE.)

JULIE. Ow!

JEN. Sorry.

JULIE. *Snorts.* Boundaries are not about a lack of intimacy, Marcus. You can be intimate and still have boundaries. Boundaries are like a gate on a bridge.

MARCUS. Who told you that? What self-help book did you yank that one out of?

JULIE. No one told me that. I don't have to be told that.

MARCUS. Okay. Look, whatever you say.

JULIE. Don't give up. What do you think?

MARCUS. I never think anything.

JULIE. Does he always do this?

JEN. Do what?

JULIE. Say something totally ridiculous and then not take responsibility for it?!

JEN. I don't … think so.

JULIE. Well it's irresponsible. And it's a terrible foundation. It's a complete lack of trust. It's like he's saying "you have no right to how I really feel, so I'll just keep that secret."

JEN. I don't think he does that. Do you do that?

MARCUS. I don't know. Sure. Whatever you say. Can we just get on with it?

JULIE. You see? He's doing it again!

MARCUS. I don't know what I'm doing!

JULIE. That is so like you.

MARCUS. Can I ask you something?

(JEN kicks MARCUS.)

JULIE. Go ahead.

(JEN kicks MARCUS.)

MARCUS. Why did they put you in charge of bridal registry? STOP KICKING ME!

JEN. Oh, was that my foot? Sorry, I —

MARCUS. No, I'm serious. Why is that? It sounds like you're totally off marriage. And you're sitting here advising happy couples what to get for their wedding? You know, everyone has got to get their licks on how we should be married. Her mother's got to tell us that a good relationship's based on trust, my father tells me to keep my secrets and keep my friends. HER Dad tells me that oral sex is key. You! I have no idea what you're telling us. What is with you people? How many people who come through this office even GET married?

JULIE. You have some serious issues, my friend. You have some serious intimacy issues. I know you. I know your type.

MARCUS. Oh you DO, do you? *(JEN kicks MARCUS.)* What?!

JEN. It's time to go.

JULIE. Now you listen to me, Mister Man.

MARCUS. Whoa!

JULIE. I give your marriage three years, tops. And I refuse to be a party to this ... this farce of a marriage. You want someone to handle this, you're going to have to go to Bed, Bath and Beyond, because I am not going to just sit here and let you —

(JEN jumps up and knocks her chair down.)

JEN. Bite me, you — !

JULIE. What?

JEN. What gives you the right? What gives you the right? Huh? Who the fuck are you? Telling us how long we'll be married? It is none of your business. So why don't you just shut up. You just — you — my mother tells me I can't marry him! You! You don't have the RIGHT. I know he's not much and there's beard hairs all over the fucking place and he walks around with stains on his shirts, but he's mine and I love him and you're bitter because you couldn't hold onto Rod. *(JULIE snorts.)* And get your nose fixed or something. Marcus we're going.

MARCUS. Told you we should have gone to Pottery Barn.

JEN. Shut up; you started this. I'm in the car. Get the ... get the stuff.

(Exit JEN.)

MARCUS. I'm sorry about all this —

JULIE. No, no. I — I'm sorry about —

(JULIE snorts and wipes at her nose.)

    MARCUS. Don't worry about it, okay?

(He hands JULIE his handkerchief.)

    JULIE. Thank you. I ought to try that Seldane stuff.
    MARCUS. They discontinued it.

(Pause)

    JULIE. I shouldn't have done that — You … you should get back to your fiancée.
    MARCUS. Yeah. Only if you're okay.
    JULIE. I'm sorry.
    MARCUS. I miss you too.
    JULIE. I never said I missed you.
    MARCUS. I know.
    JULIE. I probably should have told you about my new job.
    MARCUS. Ha. Yeah, I guess you should have.
    JULIE. I like the beard. *(Pause)* You're going to have to tell her sooner or later.
    MARCUS. I know.
    JULIE, When you get to city hall, she's gonna know.
    MARCUS. I know. In a way, I think she knows already.
    JULIE. That's not the point. You have to tell her.
    MARCUS. I know. I do.
    JULIE. Marcus, we could have —
    MARCUS. Yeah.

(Pause)

    JULIE. Keep your beard hairs out of her toothbrush, Marcus. It's really gross.
    MARCUS. I'll do what I can.
    JULIE. Do more, Marcus. Do more.

THE END

COSTUME PLOT

JEN & JULIE:
   Sweater sets and black shoes. Plain skirt

JEN:
   Simple string of pearls, matching earrings, large (but not tasteless) engagement ring

MARCUS:
   Stylish slacks, short-sleeve shirt

PROPERTY PLOT

High-end shopping bags (Barneys, Prada), Prada handbag (JEN)
Pack of cigarettes, stack of papers, pens, catalogue (JULIE)
Handkerchief (MARCUS)

SET DRAWING

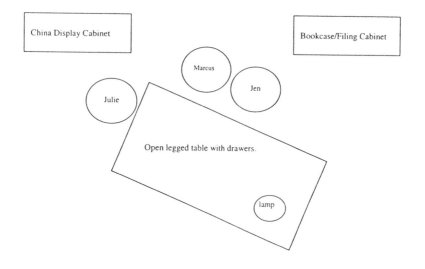

A PINK CADILLAC NIGHTMARE

by

Le Wilhelm

A PINK CADILLAC NIGHTMARE is only one of about forty one-acts which were produced in many forms over the last fifteen years. During the early inception of the plays the overall title was GRASSROOTS and the Julie character, then Tammy Lee, sold marijuana for a living. During that time, one actress week after week was learning four new one-acts. If it had not been for her dedication to the project, this and all the rest would not have come to fruition. Therefore, this play is being dedicated to Lissa Watson, who lives somewhere in Europe now.

A PINK CADILLAC NIGHTMARE was produced at the Short Play Festival by Love Creek Productions under the direction of Elizabeth Lambert. The cast was as follows:

JULIE . . . . Lee Eypper

BECKY . . . . Wende O'Reilly

Previously the show was produced with four other plays featuring the character of Julie under the title of BUBBLING, under the direction of Gregg David Shore. Other actresses over the years who have played Julie are Jackie Jenkins and Lissa Watson ... other Beckies include Ruth Harmon, Patricia Hicok, CaSandra Brooks.

ABOUT THE AUTHOR

LE WILHELM is a past festival winner who has had a number of plays published by Samuel French, including *Blackberry Frost; Cherry Blend with Vanilla; Life Comes to the Old Maid; Meridan, Mississippi, Redux; One-Eyed Venus and the Brothers; Pie Supper; The Power and the Glory; The Road to Nineveh; Strawberry Preserves; A Significant Betrayal; Tremulous* and *Whoppers*. More information on his work is available on the Internet at *www.geocities.com/lewilhelm/*.

CHARACTERS

JULIE: A nice woman. Married. Age 30ish or older.
BECKY: A Mary Kay saleswoman on the verge of hysteria. Married with children. Late 30's to 50's.

SETTING

Pink Cadillac Nightmare takes place in Julie's new and used shop. (The set need consist of nothing more than a table with two chairs, or it can be as elaborate as the producers choose).

(As the lights come up, JULIE, a woman in her thirties, is asleep in her chair. The set consists of various pieces of junk, mixed with some nice pieces. There is also a case which contains pieces of rocks and stones. Perhaps a few new age books are present and a crystal ball. This is all mixed with furniture from the not too distant past. This is "Julie's Junque and Stuff." JULIE is the operator of the establishment.)

BECKY. *(Off)* Julie! Julie!
JULIE. What?

(BECKY enters. She is a woman of high energy. She carries with her a large case which contains the tools of her trade.)

BECKY. Are you ready?
JULIE. Ready?
BECKY. Yeah.
JULIE. Ready for what, Becky?
BECKY. Don't tell me you've forgotten.
JULIE. Ah.
BECKY. Julie, I'm on a very tight schedule. You said that I could come by around two o'clock today and give you a facial.
JULIE. It plumb slipped my mind.
BECKY. Do you have anything else planned?
JULIE. Ah. Ah … no, not really.
BECKY. Great.
JULIE. Becky, I don't remember scheduling a facial —
BECKY. Well, you did.
JULIE. Whatever you say, Becky.
BECKY. I'm not lying.
JULIE. I didn't think you were, Becky.
BECKY. I'm not!
JULIE. Calm down, Becky, you just caught me by surprise.
BECKY. That's good.
JULIE. What is?
BECKY. That I caught you by surprise. A lovely surprise on this lovely afternoon. Now just sit down right here. First I'm going to clean your face.
JULIE. I can do that —
BECKY. No, no, no. I wouldn't hear of it. Besides, these little towelettes get right down to the surface. Get in the pores and clean out all

63

the dirt and grime. Not that you have dirt and grime on your face. I'm sure you're very clean. But we all do have a certain amount of dirt and grime, no matter how clean we are. And these things really get in and clean out all that guck. Can't you feel it?

JULIE. I guess.

BECKY. Course you can. Relax. You're tense.

JULIE. I'm sorry.

BECKY. Just give yourself over to a wonderful experience. Let Becky take control.

JULIE. All right.

BECKY. Today is going to be one of the most important days of your life, Julie. Mary Kay is going to change your life.

JULIE. Actually I'm a pretty happy person, Becky.

BECKY. I know. I know. But things can always be better, right? Right?

JULIE. Right.

BECKY. Now before we go any further, there are two things I must say, because legally I have to say them. First is that I am not a licensed cosmetologist. Now, I probably know more about this than most licensed cosmetologists, but I am not licensed. But since we're friends, I figure we don't have to worry about all that, right?

JULIE. Of course not, Becky.

BECKY. And the second thing is that I'm really doing something that is not right. If Mary Kay knew about this, she would string me up by my toes. I'm also giving a facial to Jane Phillips who lives the next street over —

JULIE. I know Jane.

BECKY. She's nice, isn't she?

JULIE. Yeah. She's real shy.

BECKY. At any rate, I'm giving a facial to her right as we speak, and so I have to go back over there in about twenty minutes. And then I'll come back and finish up here, if that's all right?

JULIE. Whatever.

BECKY. I'm sure glad, because Jane would get worried if I didn't make it back to take off her pack. Now Julie when you're demonstrating this stuff, you have to go through each one of the steps and explain to the customer exactly what you're doing and what the product does for their skin and for their beauty.

JULIE. Becky, I don't want to sell this stuff.

BECKY. You never know. Oh, you have such a beautiful complexion.

JULIE. I do?

BECKY. Oh yes, and if you do decide to sell this stuff, it can be a selling point. Your customers will look at your skin and think theirs is going to look like yours. They won't know you're a natural beauty. But it wouldn't matter if you had bad skin, because Mary Kay could take care of it. This stuff is good. Now I'm about to begin. You just stay relaxed, and we'll chitchat about whatever you want. Later when you get interested in having Mary Kay parties yourself, then I'll teach you how to do the whole sales approach.

JULIE. I don't want to sell cosmetics. Not that there's anything wrong with it, but I couldn't.

BECKY. That's a mistake. "Couldn't" doesn't exist in our vocabulary. And besides, you would be a fantastic salesperson.

JULIE. What on earth makes you say that?

BECKY. You got tons of friends always dropping by to see you. You could just mention that you happen to sell Mary Kay.

JULIE. That's just not me, Becky. I'd feel guilty.

BECKY. You just got to adapt, and I figure you're like me and have a high degree of adaptability. I pride myself on my adaptability, and I'm sure you do, too. And besides, Julie, a lot of your close friends are women our age, right?

JULIE. Sure.

BECKY. They're at the age when they're beginning to notice the crows' feet. The gray hairs. Women our age are just like ripe fruit, overripe fruit, ready to be plucked.

JULIE. Is that how you see me, Becky? As a big aging overripe piece of fruit that you're about ready to pick?

BECKY. Of course not. We're friends. If I were trying to pluck you, Julie, I wouldn't be telling you all this, now would I?

JULIE. No, I don't guess so.

BECKY. Of course not.

JULIE. But I'm not selling cosmetics.

BECKY. Okay. I won't pester you. But the profits are great. Bathroom's back there, right?

JULIE. Uh huh.

BECKY. I'm going to get some warm water.

JULIE. I'll —

BECKY. *(Going for the water.)* Nonsense, you just sit back and be a queen. Let me take care of everything.

JULIE. All right.

BECKY. Have you ever had a facial before?

JULIE. Once.

BECKY. Oh?

JULIE. In Kansas City.

BECKY. What kind was it?

JULIE. A mud pack.

BECKY. Did you like it?

JULIE. It was okay.

BECKY. Well, this one's going to be great.

JULIE. Why are you so hot on trying to sign people up to sell Mary Kay?

BECKY. I haven't been pushy about it, have I?

JULIE. No ... I just wondered what's in it for you.

BECKY. Pink Cadillac.

JULIE. Huh?

BECKY. Pink Cadillac is what you get if you're real successful with Mary Kay.

JULIE. They give their salespeople pink Cadillacs.

BECKY. Honey, I'm not just a salesperson anymore. I've moved up the Mary Kay ladder. I'm a director. I got lots of folks working for me. I just signed up Daphne Dumas. You know her, don't you?

JULIE. Oh sure.

BECKY. I think she'll be great. Lots of your friends and neighbors are selling Mary Kay. But to get a pink Cadillac free, you have to be more than just a salesperson. That's where you should set your long range sights. A directorship, and if you don't want a pink Cadillac, you can take a real nice fur coat instead. Me, I want the Caddy. And I wouldn't advise anyone to bet against me.

JULIE. I wouldn't.

BECKY. You know me. And when I get that car, I'm going to drive up and down these streets, honking and waving at everyone. And then I'm going to drive up Elm Street where Richard and I used to live, and I'm going to lay on the horn from one end of it to the other. Give them rich people something to —

JULIE. You be careful, they'll turn you in for disturbance of the peace.

BECKY. Let them. Won't be the first time. I don't care, I'll pay the fine. It'd be worth it. Course the police ain't so likely to ticket you if you're driving a Caddy. 'Sides, if I have that Caddy, I'll have plenty of money and so I won't care if I get the ticket.

JULIE. You make good money selling —

BECKY. The best. And the more salespeople I have out there selling, the more money I make.

JULIE. Sounds like you got plenty of people selling for you. There ain't that many people in this town.

BECKY. A lot of people live out in the countryside, too. And those women enjoy having someone come and visit. Doesn't this feel wonderful? Can't you just feel your skin relaxing, revitalizing, rejuvenating, restructuring, reinvigorating?

JULIE. It does feel good.

BECKY. It's a real hoot, how they discovered the formula for this cream.

JULIE. Oh?

BECKY. Uh huh.

JULIE. How did they discover the formula?

BECKY. There's this old geezer who was a hide tanner out in Texas.

Now this old guy starts noticing that his hands aren't aging like the rest of his body. So he puts two and two together and starts putting the tanning solution on his face.

JULIE. Really?

BECKY. Uh huh. And his face starts looking younger. He was around sixty years òld, and he looked like he was forty. His daughter notices this and so she tries it, too, and his daughter, she was into Stanley products.

JULIE. I remember those. Their spices were really good. Momma used to always get those from the Stanley man. She said they had the best orange and lemon extracts that there —

BECKY. His daughter starts using all her Stanley customers as guinea pigs, having them all use this tanning ointment.

JULIE. Is this true?

BECKY. Yes.

JULIE. I don't know about that, Becky. I don't know if I believe women would put something like tanning oil on their face when they don't know if it'll work or not.

BECKY. Honey, believe it. Women will put anything on their face, or anywhere else, if they think it's going to bring them eternal youth. Doesn't this feel good?

JULIE. You know, it really does.

BECKY. Of course it does. And Julie, you know it's important to treat yourself special every once in a while. That's something I've had to learn. Now, Mary Kay Ash, who is the founder of the company — that's how Mary Kay got its name, from her — Mary Kay Ash —

JULIE. I see.

BECKY. And Mary Kay saw all these women at the Stanley party who had healthy luxurious skin, and ten years later she's in business. All she really did to the tanning ointment is to make it smell better. Put some perfume or something in it to keep it from stinking.

JULIE. It smells alright.

BECKY. Of course it does. Mary Kay wouldn't have it any other way. And you know what's wonderful about the company is that it focuses on helping women. Last year I did so well, I got to go to the big national convention. Went right to Mary Kay's house … and oh, Julie, it is palatial. Palatial is what it is.

JULIE. Real nice, huh

BECKY. Palatial.

JULIE. Sounds like she's making a mint.

BECKY. And why shouldn't she.

JULIE. No reason.

BECKY. No reason at all. Look what she's doing for the women of the world. Hell, Julie, I was skeptical when I first started out. Just did it hoping to make a few extra bucks after Richard's injury. We got his Social Security with some compensation, but it just wasn't enough. Not with the kids. So I had to try something. And at first I read the material, and I thought the Mary Kay women were real weirdos. But I was desperate. And then I found out they're not weirdos, Not at all. They're just living the American Dream. And the incentives are great.

JULIE. Sounds like you're really —

BECKY. The best. Pink cadillacs, furs, jewels. And I love what Mary Kay says about the pink Cadillac!

JULIE. What's that?

BECKY. *(Produces a pamphlet and reads.)* "So you think a pink Cadillac's tacky? What other company gives you a free car?"

JULIE. She does have a point.

BECKY. Me, I don't think a pink Cadillac's tacky. And so what if it is. I like pink flamingos. And my bathroom's painted pink, with a pink stool cover and pink towels and a pink throw rug — I love pink!

JULIE. Careful, don't get that stuff in my eyes.

BECKY. Sorry. I just get carried away when I talk about Mary Kay.

JULIE. Monique gets the same way when she discusses her boutique. She got a Small Business Loan.

BECKY. That's wonderful. She'd be a great one to sell Mary Kay. You know, when Richard got hurt we lost our house on Elm Street, and you know those people that lived there didn't have a kind word to say to us. That's why I can't wait to drive down that street honking my horn at them. Julie, I want to tell you something, but it's real personal, and you have to promise not to laugh at me.

JULIE. I promise.

BECKY. When I was in Dallas, I had an experience that was … it was like one of those psychic things they talk about on television, those Time-Life books they were selling a while back. You remember that ad where they keep repeating the phrase, "Read the book?"

JULIE. Uh huh.

BECKY. I was in Dallas, in the toilet — I had just finished taking a whiz — and was washing my hands, and guess who walks in?

JULIE. Who?

BECKY. Mary Kay Ash herself. And she comes up and stands beside me and starts washing her hands just like I was doing. The bathroom had two separate sinks. It was a pink bathroom — like mine. Then she smiles at me and says, "I bet you're a dynamite sales person." She said that. And then she said, "Next year, I expect to see you on stage getting your pink Cadillac." Julie, my flesh tingled when she said that, and I swear there was light all around her. And you know, she was right. I am going to be there. I am.

JULIE. Sounds like an epiphany.

BECKY. I don't know about that. I just know I'd do anything short of killing to get my Caddy.

JULIE. Becky, you want to be careful.

BECKY. Careful?

JULIE. You don't want to put yourself under too much pressure.

BECKY. Julie, I want to be a productive member of society. I got married when I was sixteen, and I always thought all I could do was raise kids and cook. But I know now that's not true. And I'm happy. It's true that sometimes I have trouble sleeping, but I'm happy.

JULIE. You can't sleep?

BECKY. Just a little problem. Nothing to even talk about. Now this is the last part of the facial.

JULIE. Just don't push yourself too hard, honey.

BECKY. This is the stuff that I think feels so good.

JULIE. You're not sleeping?

BECKY. Ever since Mary Kay and I met in the toilet, I've had some trouble. Nothing to talk about. This is great, isn't it?

JULIE. It does feel good. Do you have any idea why you can't sleep?

BECKY. I used to always count sheep. But not anymore. After that meeting, all I see is pink Cadillacs. One comes over the hill, passes, and then another. That's how it started. Then I start seeing Mary Kay herself sitting behind the steering wheel. Then she starts waving. And that's nice. Then she starts honking at me. That ain't so good. I'm just drifting off, and Mary Kay drives by in one of her Caddies, waves, and then she honks. Now she's starting to talk to me. Say things.

JULIE. Like what?

BECKY. Just smiles and says, "Wouldn't you like to have this car?" or "See you in Dallas!" And then she honks. It's that goddamn honking that's driving me nuts. I've tried everything, but nothing works.

JULIE. I'm telling you you're pushing too hard. Bobby Joe does the same thing. He takes on too much and then when he gets a break, he can't sleep. Or has these terrible nightmares about jackknifing and all sorts of horrible things. You've got to slow down.

BECKY. Slow down? How the hell am I ever going to get that car if I slow down???!!! I'm in the top ten percent in the region. I've already made enough this year to pay the tuition for my Roy. It's his senior year in college. I'm getting new furniture … if she'd just stop honking life would be great. This is all finished. Now, let's see what time it is. Now you just sit there and enjoy yourself and don't move around. Whoops. I've got to run.

JULIE. This feels great.

BECKY. I'll be back in about thirty minutes.

JULIE. What?

BECKY. I have to go back over to Jane's. I told you about that. Now just relax.

JULIE. Is this stuff safe to leave on your face indefinitely?

BECKY. It's fine for up to thirty minutes.

JULIE. Then what?

BECKY. We don't need to talk about that. I'll be back. I'll bring back my case which has all the beauty products. And information about being a salesperson.

JULIE. What if you don't get back in thirty minutes?

BECKY. I will! I will.

JULIE. But if you don't.

BECKY. You can wash it off. But don't worry.

JULIE. Becky, this makes me nervous.

BECKY. Julie, I'll be back. It's only a couple of blocks away. Just close your eyes, relax, feel yourself becoming young again. All of us women got to learn to treat ourselves better. Now just relax, breathe deeply and think how great it would be driving a pink Cadillac.

(JULIE does so, as BECKY exits.)

JULIE. Becky? Becky? Oh, Jesus. I don't even like pink.

(Lights out.)

COSTUME PLOT

Contemporary; Becky should definitely have a lot of pink in her costume.

PROPERTY PLOT

A satchel that looks like a makeup seller's display kit
Makeup to apply facial
Bowl for water
Facial tissues
Pads
Etc.

SET DRAWING

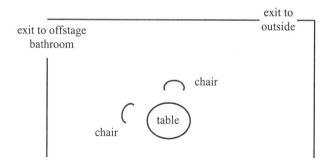

NOTE: The floor plan is simple. The play has been intentionally written in such a way as to allow it to be performed with a minimal set. Above are the necessary elements

EAST OF THE SUN
AND WEST OF THE MOON

by

Peter Handy

This play is dedicated to
Erica Silberman, my "Miss Nurse,"
my teachers, the artists who have inspired me,
my friends and my family.

EAST OF THE SUN AND WEST OF THE MOON was presented at the Off-Off-Broadway Original Short Play Festival on July 14 -16, 2000, under the direction of Kevin Kittle with the following cast:

CONSTANCE .... Erica Silberman
MICHAEL .... Frank Shattuck

ABOUT THE AUTHOR

Born and raised in Manhattan, PETER HANDY has always felt more at peace away from the city in nature. He completed two Outward Bound courses as a teenager and, while working with a research group whose concern was the protection of the grizzly bear habitat outside of Yellowstone National Park, he learned Native American survival techniques. In New York City he studied modern dance, acting and creative writing before attending Sarah Lawrence College, where he wrote short stories and plays, made short films, choreographed and acted in a number of theatrical productions. He has since lived in Norway for two years and, upon his return to New York, studied acting with Maggie Flannigan, Deborah Hedwall, Tim Phillips and Wynn Handman and writing with Curt Dempster. He has worked as an actor and a writer with The Ensemble Studio Theatre, All Seasons Theatre, Naked Angels, The Image Theatre, The Workshop at The Neighborhood Playhouse and The Cherry Lane Alternative.

CHARACTERS

MICHAEL ZIEGLER (Walking Bear): a wounded Wold War I soldier
CONSTANCE BILLINGS (Miss Nurse): a British army nurse

SETTING

Place: A ward in an army hospital in Flanders, a train crossing the American West, an Indian reservation in South Dakota, London Square, a ship crossing the ocean, and others
Time: World War I

(A ward in a World War I army hospital in Flanders. In the center of the upstage wall, one cot, cot-side table and stool are seen. Stage left are a writing desk and a chair. Stage right is a wooden box or crate.)

(The pre-show music, popular songs from World War I played at a low volume, should lead into a particular, well-chosen song, which begins the transition into the play. The volume should come up a bit as the house lights fade to half, then to black.)

(The characters then take their places on the stage. MICHAEL, an American Indian, takes his place on the cot. CONSTANCE, a British army nurse, takes her place at the desk. Stage lights fade up to reveal CONSTANCE writing a letter. MICHAEL, in shadow, is lying asleep under a sheet on the cot. His head and eyes are heavily bandaged.)

(The music fades out a beat or two after the stage lights come up and then CONSTANCE begins her letter.)

CONSTANCE.
From the 52nd regimental mobile field hospital, Flanders
October 11th, 1917

Dear Mother and Father,
    Thank you both for your lovely package. It arrived here this morning. Thank you for such a thoughtful and supportive letter, Mother; and thank you, Father, for the wonderful gift of our favorite fairy tale. The story takes me back to my childhood, to the comfort of being held by you, and to our evenings together reading it by the fireplace. Which reminds me ...
    Please give my love to Philip. He didn't respond to my last letter. If he is still cross with me, tell him that I love him and miss him very much and can hardly wait for this war to be over so I can come home and marry him. Oh, and tell him that I saw Peter Davies the other day. His company was passing through on their way to the front. He was bright and cheerful and telling jokes with the doctors in the mess hall. He even had Dr. Gallagher in stitches, so to speak. Sadly, his company left for the front yesterday morning. What else shall I tell you.... Oh yes, here's some interesting news, one of the soldiers who came in with a bad head wound is an American Indian named Ziegler. Isn't that marvelously queer and ironic, an American Indian with a German name? In any case, according to Dr. Gallagher, he was lucky the bullet didn't hit his helmet more directly or Mr. Ziegler would now be in heaven, or wherever Indians go. Dr. Gallagher wasn't sure that Mr. Ziegler was going to pull through, so I spent much of the night until early morning making sure he was still breathing.
    Speaking of morning, I need to check on my soldiers now. Please do

not worry about gas attacks. The field unit is well equipped to take proper precautions, and so far none of us have been harmed.

Send me more news about you and Pam. Is that American soldier still courting her? I promise I'll write you soon.

Your loving daughter,
Constance

(Music and light cue: Lyrical music, with the feeling of early morning, fades in as CONSTANCE folds the letter, gets up taking the book with her from the desk, and moves upstage to the cot where MICHAEL, slightly propped up, is lying. The lights fade out on Constance's desk and come up on Michael's cot as CONSTANCE reaches it.)

CONSTANCE. Good morning Private Ziegler. Michael Ziegler, Jr., isn't that an odd Indian name? *(She goes to look at the dogtags around his neck.)* I wonder what your real name is. *(He tries to speak, but it comes out in a hoarse whisper.)* Oh, shh! Don't try to speak. You were shot. We operated on you last night. You will have to stay here for a few weeks, and Dr. Gallagher has given me strict orders not to let you speak until things have had time to heal up a bit. *(He tries to speak again.)* Shh! Here. *(She gently takes his hand.)* Can you squeeze my hand? *(He squeezes her hand.)* Good, that's it. This is how we will talk for now. Squeeze one time for yes, two times for no. Do you know where you are? *(He squeezes her hand once, etc.)* You do? Good. Do you understand what has happened to you? Good. Do you remember me singing to you last night? Yes. Good. The doctor said you were very lucky. He is reasonably sure you will have a full recovery. Are you glad to hear that? Oh, you are. Good, I was glad to hear that too. In a few days we will take the bandages off and you can write me notes. I think that will be great fun, don't you? *(He squeezes her hand twice, etc.)* You don't. You don't? Are you playing with me? Good. I thought so. Later, if you're nice, I can read to you when I have time. That way I won't prattle on and you won't die of boredom. Well that's enough for now. Try to rest up a bit.

(As she turns to go, he reaches out for her and faintly whispers.)

MICHAEL. Miss Nurse!
CONSTANCE. Shh!
MICHAEL. *(Whispers.)* Read!
CONSTANCE. Do you want me to read to you now? You do. *(She gently places his hand back down on his chest and gets the stool, takes the book from the table and sits down to read to him.)* Alright then, here's a good story. It's a fairy tale called East of the Sun and West of the Moon. It's about a bear who takes a young girl on a long journey and saves her

and her family from a life of poverty. "Once long ago there lived a husband and his wife and their seven children. They had not enough to eat, *(His hand reaches up for hers and holds it until she finishes the fairy tale.)* and their clothes were patched and worn because they were poor. The seven children were all quite beautiful despite their ragged clothing, but the loveliest of them all was the youngest daughter, who was as breathtaking as the first spring flowers."

(Music and light cue: Rhythmical, possibly Native American music fades in as MICHAEL sits up and CONSTANCE stylistically unwinds Michael's bandage as if releasing him from weeks of being under her care. The lights fade out on the cot and come up on the wooden crate as MICHAEL slowly makes his way to the crate to begin his first letter. CONSTANCE, now in shadow, cleans up the cot and surrounding area after MICHAEL has left. She doesn't move back to her desk until about the time MICHAEL says, "I'm travelin on the railroad now.")
(Two months later.)

MICHAEL. *(Before he sits down:)*
December 13, 1917

(He sits down on the crate, picks up pencil and paper, and begins by writing:)
Dear Miss Nurse,
(He repeats it and takes it out to the audience:)
Dear Miss Nurse,
Here's the letter you are more than deservin of and asked me to send for your knowin of my well bein. I know I left the soldier infirmary earlier than you reckoned was wise but the army doctor who saw my head wound said it was healin up real good. Anyways, I showed him the "reddish tint" from the infection you was concerned bout an he made a joke, on account of my bein a "Red Indian," how could he see for the difference. But he said you was right to be carin bout it cause head wounds can be a tricky thing.
I want you to know that I needed to go cause my family was waitin and I knows they could use my army pay real bad.
You was right. I received an honorable discharge and a purple heart for servin my country. The purple heart keeps me from bein shameful for not being able to fight no more.

(Light cue: The stage lights gradually come up to half on Constance's desk as she crosses downstage from the cot.)

I'm travelin on the railroad now. Gonna reach the border of my homeland South Dakota a bit before nightfall.
Comin back to the hills and rivers I know so well by means of the "iron horse" gives me a sorrowful feelin; tomorrow, I'll be glad to be travelin by foot and horse from the train station back to the reservation.

Anyways, I know this will make me happy.
(Michael's voice segues to Constance's voice reading his letter, i.e. his voice fades out as her voice fades in reading the exact same words.)
(Light cue: The stage lights gradually come up to full on Constance's desk as she begins to speak.)

CONSTANCE.
Anyways, I know this will make me happy. Sometimes when I walk alone softly I see the places I have visited and they feel like places I know from my dreams. When I sleep alone on the open land I feel closer in my heart to where I am. I see the world. I hear the voices in all things and I know everythin I need to know. I am grateful. I am happy.

Tomorrow morning I'm gonna pass a post station in Sioux City an send this letter to you so you will know I'm doin fine.

Ah geez, I been callin you Miss Nurse for so long I really don't remember your "given name," so I'll just send it to you as Miss Nurse and hope it finds you.

Michael Ziegler Jr.

Since you was wonderin, the name Michael Ziegler was given to my father when he was moved to the reservation. There ain't no rhyme nor reason for it.

My tribal name is Walking Bear

(CONSTANCE begins reciting/writing a letter to MICHAEL here.)

Jan. 9th, 1918

Dear Michael Ziegler, Jr.,
Today your letter finally arrived at my desk. Have you really forgotten my name or are you playing the trickster once again? If so it was very naughty of you not to use my given name on the envelope, Michael, because your letter was opened and passed from person to person until someone remembered you and realized the letter must be for me.

I am still cross with you for leaving before you were fully recovered. There could be bone fragments from the bullet loose in your skull. Of course the doctor told you you were well enough to travel. From his point of view, we need every available bed for white soldiers. I understand that your family wants you home again, and you want to share your money with them, but it was foolish of you not to heed my advice. Please seek the best medical treatment you can and have your wound taken care of.

On a lighter note, your description of South Dakota has transported me out of this nightmare … for the time being.

I eagerly await your next letter.

Sincerely yours,
Constance "Miss Nurse"

P.S. Thank you for sharing your tribal name with me. May I address you as Walking Bear in future salutations?

MICHAEL.
In the middle of the Moon of the Popping Trees "December"

Dear Constance,
    I finally remembered your name. I'm afraid the other letter I sent you will get lost over there so I'm sending this one for you by way of your "given name" right away. Anyways I likes writin you letters, it makes me feel nearer to you.
    I've made it most of the way to the reservation now an I'm camped out alone in a grove surrounded by cottonwoods. I got a fire goin and dug out the shelter and laid out some fresh buffalo grass to sleep on. My hands and feet are steamin warm from the fire and my heart feels open and calm.
    I done heard the wolves howlin as the moon came over the hills. I seen my old, old trees an the rocks that I know an can see the rollin plains that look like big, long, snowy waves in the moonlight. In the stories I heard from my elders, the great spirit Wankan Tanka feels us on his back. I feel at home here like I'm layin on what you'd call God's back. I know you know what I'm sayin.
    Tomorrow I'm gonna be home with all my relations. We call this "Mitakuya Oyasin." It means "all my relations."

(CONSTANCE repeats "Mitakuya Oyasin" and then begins reading his letter out loud.)

CONSTANCE.
Mitakuya Oyasin.
    I'm sendin you a map so you can see where I live. It's the Lower Brule reservation an its where the Missouri turns back on itself in an S. "Oh!" *(CONSTANCE finds the place on Michael's map which was pre-set on her desk.)* That's where I'm gonna be tomorrow. My father, my mother an my uncle Eldon Teeton now live there. I am feelin very tired an will now sleep by my fire. I'll write more about my homecomin later.

Hope you is well,
Walking Bear

(To herself:) So he really didn't remember my name. *(She begins her letter.)*
Dear Michael Walking Bear,
    I was so excited to receive more news from you.
    I have to say it is as much a torture as a relief to read your beautiful letter. I would have loved to have been camped out where you were and to have seen the land stretching out in front of me. No people, just land.
    It comforts me to know that you are back in the land you love so much.

Things here are very busy. I rarely sleep more than four hours a night, and I get to forgetting that I am alive. Now your letters remind me of what is important. They calm me as you did when you were here. When the front is quiet, I listen to the sounds around me more clearly. Sometimes birds sing and the war seems completely crazy. Other times the silence feels so deep I suddenly awake as if from a dream and see the wounded and the dead with new eyes.

It is all so sad, but it is so real.

Constance

MICHAEL.
Dear Constance,
I wish't you'd been here to see when I got back to the reservation. My family has moved into long tents with kerosene stoves a good bit nearer to the Missouri River. When I walked up my mother came out and looked at me for a long time an said nothin but had tears in her eyes. My father stared at his feet an laughed an got out his pipe to share with me. The Chief, Noah Grassrope, took me by the hand an gave me a red eagle feather. An then my uncle, Eldon Teeton, came up an shook my hand an says, "Hey grandson howdja get that scratch on your head, was you choppin wood with a dull ax or somethin?"

My relations ask me about the war very little, but they honor me in our traditional way. They dance the mornin wind dance for warriors who come back from battle wounded cause the mornin wind on the waters renews the life spirit. Since I had just come from the east we prayed to the risin sun and the early mornin winds on the lakes.

(CONSTANCE finishes reading his letter.)

CONSTANCE.
Then we dance the next night the Neebiche dance, meanin the leaves that are blown an drift before the wind in the empty forest. This is the dance of changin times because they have to take me back into their circle now.

My uncle Eldon Teeton says we have a lot of wind dances here because we eat too many beans.

Mitakuya Oyasan
This is a prayer that we will be reunited one day.

Walking Bear

(CONSTANCE begins letter to him here.)

Dear Walking Bear,
Two soldiers from your troop stopped by to ask about you today. Marc Eaton and John Wymen are their names. They said you were a great

soldier. They said you were fearless and, that the day you were wounded, you saved another soldier's life by diverting gunfire in your direction when he fell down. They said it was the bravest thing they'd ever seen a man do. They wish you the best in America.

Michael, I hope you will continue to write when time allows.

Yours with great admiration,
Constance

(Pause and music cue: Tender, but rhythmically upbeat, music fades in as CONSTANCE gets up, walks upstage and back around her desk to discover the box which was pre-set containing Michael's presents to her.)

MICHAEL. My mother dream't of you in a white dress bringin me back home to her. I told her how, on that night the gray-haired doctor took the bullet out of my skull, you held my hand through the night and sang that song to me. She says you have as much courage as I do.

CONSTANCE. Your mother gives me too much credit in her dream. I was just doing my job.

MICHAEL. My father sent that blanket cause he knows how it is to be too cold. I told him how there wasn't enough blankets for the soldiers. He says to tell you that his name is Michael Ziegler Sr. I told him you know that already. My mother sent that pouch, it was a weddin present from her mother who died at Wounded Knee. I filled it with dried sweet grass.

CONSTANCE. The gifts you sent are lovely. I kept the blanket for myself. I couldn't bear to part with it.

MICHAEL. I've been workin on my letter writing with the new teacher we have. She is worried bout the wound in my head and thought that I should tell you.

CONSTANCE. She is quite right to be concerned about your health. Do you spend much time with this teacher. Is she pretty?... *(She crosses "pretty" out.)* Is she sweet?

MICHAEL. She's an old fat nun that the children make fun of cause she smells bad.

CONSTANCE. Well that's not nice.

MICHAEL. Miss Nurse ...

CONSTANCE. Please address me as Constance.

MICHAEL. Constance. I had this dream you *was* in. I woke up in a dream this mornin and you *was* sittin on the side of my bed ...

CONSTANCE. *(Correcting his English.)* "*Were* sitting on the side of your bed!"

MICHAEL. You were sittin on the side of my bed. Then from behind you in the doorway I saw the ghost of my old friend Daniel. He was wavin at me as if he wanted me to follow him somewhere, an I could tell you wanted me to stay, but I followed him anyways.

(CONSTANCE and MICHAEL look at each other through these next two lines.)

CONSTANCE. You see, even in your dreams you are stubborn.

MICHAEL. I know. Anyways, I followed him westward through the snow till we came to the Black Hills and we climbed up to the top of this hilltop and we was standing there together lookin around at the land all lit up below us from the full moon in the east. I could see Harney Peak far to the south of us and all of a sudden the sky started to glow brighter. We stood there and watched as the mornin light overtook the moon. But then I noticed that the sky was growin bright from the wrong side of the slope I was on and suddenly the sun started risin up, backwards like, out of the west. I looked behind me and the moon was settin in the east. Then I remembered that story you read to me that I liked so much. I closed my eyes and there was all these bells ringin in my head and when I opened them again I could see this big, wide street with all these tall buildings built of stone lined up around it. And the street was filled with lots of people shoutin and screamin like they was glad, and for a moment I saw you there and stood by you, and then Daniel called to me from the top of the Black Hills and I was carried away by the wind and it felt like I was flyin and then I don't remember nothin after that. But when I woke up I felt … lost. It's kinda like I don't remember where I left somethin important.

CONSTANCE. What do you think that is?

MICHAEL. I think it is you.

CONSTANCE. Well I'm glad you woke up when you did. *(Pause.)* Michael, why didn't you listen to me when I asked you to stay?

MICHAEL. I had a feelin if I didn't go home when I did I'd never see my family again.

CONSTANCE. I understand. *(Pause.)* Last night I made up my mind to leave nursing after the war ends.

MICHAEL. Why would you do somethin like that?

CONSTANCE. Peter Davies, an old friend of mine from home. A boy my fiancé, Philip, and I grew up with. He died last night. I couldn't even give him some morphine to ease his pain …

MICHAEL. Don't quit nursin! I know you eased that man's sufferin when he died. You have eased mine, even from across the ocean. I read a little part of your letter to my family and friends around the fire. I wanted them to know what you are goin through over there. We laugh at how I call you Miss Nurse. All the Indians calls you Miss Nurse. My mother and some other womens I know talk about how strong you is, how you see things with your heart not just your head. How you knew how to handle my stubbornness at comin home too early. They was saying how you is like a Lokata woman in your heart. They have respect for you and what you do. Cause you have cared for me you will always be welcome here. You are one of us.

CONSTANCE. Thank you for telling me that, Michael. Please thank your family and friends for the kick in the britches. However, it's not just Peter's death. I had a mishap one night a few weeks ago when I was sent to the front to assist Dr. Howard after a gas barrage.

We were just west of Soissons, and the destruction there was the worst we had ever seen. Bodies lay about everywhere. We looked for a pulse, a trace of breath, some sort of movement, but we found nothing. At last Dr. Howard and I split up because he thought we could cover more ground separately.

It was then that a green flair went up on the German side. I was crawling on my hands and knees when I stumbled upon the rim of this enormous crater. The flair gave me just enough light to peer into the darkness below, and there, lying at the bottom, was this soldier. His gas mask was still on and, in the shadows, I thought I saw his hand move. I called out to him, and though he didn't respond, I decided to go down and have a better look anyway. As I neared the soldier, my breathing became more and more laboured. I was reaching out to get his attention when I realized that his torso had been completely severed across the middle, and his body lay in two separate pieces. Just as a wave of nausea came over me, I felt a burning sensation in my nose and throat. I got to my feet as quickly as I could, climbed out of the crater and began to cry out for help.

It took some time before the doctors came and I was brought back to the mobile unit. I've waited, hoping the burning would go away, but it hasn't. The doctors tell me there must have been some residual gas left in the crater. They don't know what will happen to me, they're not sure if it will ever go away. So I suppose it's mostly just an inconvenience and I will get used to it, but it has coloured my perception of things for the moment, and I'm finding it very difficult to be strong now.

MICHAEL. Dear Constance, I'm tryin to look for the right words to give you. The words that will help you know how deservin you are of feelin safe. I know words have the power to heal the spirit cause your words have healed mine. But there comes a time when all words are just words and all you can do is pray and I want you to know that that is what I'm doing for you. That is what my people are doing for you. The word has traveled around Brule and all the people are singing and dancing to your name and your spirit.

CONSTANCE. Michael, thank you for your kind letter. I'm feeling a bit better. I'm sending you a present. I have to be brief. Things are very busy here right now.

(CONSTANCE signs the book on her desk as MICHAEL reaches back and finds the same book, a duplicate, pre-set in the back of his crate.)

MICHAEL. Dear Constance, I received the package with your book. Thank you for sendin it to me. I know your father used to read it to you and it has a lot of meaning to you. This is a very kind gift. I read it a lot and look at the pictures and think about you. Sometimes I read it out loud to my uncle Eldon Teeton's grandchildren before they go to sleep. I tell them how you read it to me that first morning after my operation. The children like the pictures of the bear, they say it looks just like me. We all thank you.

CONSTANCE. Michael, I have some news for you. I have a younger sister named Pamela who is engaged to an American soldier. Well, they are now going to get married, and my sister asked me if I wanted to travel with them to Ohio to help her set up her home after the wedding in London. I agreed to do it, and I have been entertaining the idea of coming to visit you. I see from the map that South Dakota is not too far from Ohio.

MICHAEL. You is welcome here. We'd be honored to receive you.

CONSTANCE. Good, then it's official! My departure date depends only on their wedding and the end of the war. Of course I have to write my fiancé Philip regarding my interest in visiting you. Keep your fingers crossed.

MICHAEL. I got more than my fingers crossed. I'm lookin forward to your comin this way real bad and hope to show you how my people live.

CONSTANCE. I would love to see how your people live.

MICHAEL. Write soon, Constance.

CONSTANCE. You too Michael. I look forward to your next letter. By the way, I keep them all in a box by my bed ... desk. With ... fondest regards, Constance.

MICHAEL. I look forward to your visit. Sincerely, Walking Bear.

(Pause and music cue: Music which suggests Philip's world in England fades in as CONSTANCE finds the envelope containing Philip's letter, which was pre-set under her lantern. She opens it, unfolds it, and begins to read.)

CONSTANCE.
From the desk of Philip Kingsbury
Sept. 1st, 1918

Dear Constance,

I received your letter regarding your interest in postponing our wedding until after your, what shall I call it, pilgrimage to South Dakota. What a novel idea. I think it's simply brilliant. I've been thinking of heading to the South Pole myself for sometime, and I think this trip of yours will allow me enough time for such an excursion. Ah! Better yet, I'll go to the North Pole. You will spend Christmas with the Indians in South Dakota, and I shall be with Santa Claus and his elves at the North Pole; and when we get back, we will both have tea with the Easter Bunny. Constance, what are you thinking? Have you gone mad? Has the war unhinged your good judgement. Yes, I have come, my little lady, to chide.

I think we understand one another quite well, Miss Billings. You know what your duties are, and you know you must come to your senses. You must have some sense that such a trip will never happen and is merely a fancy hallucination you have concocted in order to get though the war. I understand how hard it has been on you there, and I feel nothing but compassion for your endeavours to help people. You know that I, too, have made sacrifices for the war.

However, what I cannot comprehend is why you should feel so much more compelled to help strangers than to comply with the wishes of your family and closest childhood friends. You know I despise melodrama, but I think the time has come to tell you my feelings. As you know, we both have already lost enough to this bloody war. When the news of Peter's death reached home, we were all completely shattered. What shall we do without you here to mend our broken hearts? I want to love you as no other can, and I want to help you too. I want to give you beautiful things and adventures. You know that. You know that I, too, am a romantic at heart.

Please, darling, I can't bear to think of you alone and in danger anymore. I fret for your life, for your safety, every single day. Each morning that I wake up, I hope the war will be over so I can see your beautiful face. If you should leave me again, I think I shall go insane. You know I would be there, too, if it weren't for my bad leg. Please don't think me too much of a coward for telling you all this.

Love Philip

Dear Michael,
    It is true the war is winding down very quickly. Everybody knows the Germans could surrender any day.
    I have to be honest with you. I wrote my fiancé, Philip, as promised, and received his response. Philip disapproves of such a trip. If I go to visit you, he says he will break off the engagement. My mother and father are very concerned at this. They want me to marry him as soon as possible and live with him in London. Apparently they are plotting to rid themselves of both their daughters in a joint wedding as soon as the war ends. I feel very torn, and I am thinking that I might not be able to make it there now. I am sorry.

    MICHAEL.
Dear Constance,
    Here's a photograph of me in my traditional clothing. It's how I'd like you to see me right now. I owe you my life. I wish to see you again and am understanding that you have obligations to your relations and the man you're engaged to. But I won't lie to you, as a man I have feelins for you too.

(CONSTANCE picks up Michael's picture which is preset on her desk.)

CONSTANCE. Michael, thank you for your beautiful picture. I cherish it. *(Silence from MICHAEL.)* Michael, I haven't heard from you. *(Silence from MICHAEL.)* Michael, it's been over a month since I've received any mail from you. Is everything all right? *(Silence from MICHAEL.)* Michael, I haven't heard from you. Did you receive my last letter? I miss your letters terribly. *(Silence from MICHAEL.)* Michael, what is going on over there? I haven't heard anything from you in six weeks. I can only hope you are in good health. What is going on? Are you cross with me? *(Silence from MICHAEL.)*

MICHAEL.
Dear Constance,
    I'm sorry I haven't written you sooner. I didn't mean to upset you. I been very sick and trying to get the proper treatment. Been travelin to Sioux City and Pierre. Wasn't here to receive your letters. One morning I woke up and my whole left side had gone dead. I can't move or feel nothin with it now and I can't see so good with my left eye.
    I was turned away from the army hospital, they says I'm no longer a soldier. The Bureau of Indian Affairs finally sent a doctor. He says it's brain damage from the head wound, he can't do nothin for me. I can see from by mother's face that she's frightened. I'm praying and hopin you can come.

Love Michael

CONSTANCE. Michael, I have made a terrible mistake. I will come and visit you as soon as I can be released. I've told my parents there will be no joint wedding. They'll have to be satisfied with marrying off just one daughter for now. They don't understand. It's very confusing. I am sorry. We'll see what we can do when I get there. It won't be long now.
    MICHAEL. We pray for your comin.

CONSTANCE.
November 11th, 1918
Michael, the war is over.
    I'm standing in London Square as bells ring out in victory. As luck would have it, I was released from my duties a few days ago and made it home in time for my sister's wedding. I am not waiting for my sister and her husband to go to Ohio. I'm leaving on the next transatlantic liner, the day after tomorrow, and heading straight away to South Dakota to see you. *(Pause.)*

November 18th, 1918
Michael, I am crossing the Atlantic Ocean now.
    I saw Philip for the last time at my sister's wedding. I broke off the engagement for good. Needless to say he is quite angry with me, and so is

my family. They all think that I'm suffering from the effects of the war, and, that if I'm just patient, I shall return to myself in no time; but I have never felt so certain that what I am doing is the right thing. Be strong, it will not be long now before we are able to stand face to face once again. *(Pause.)*

December 3rd, 1918

Michael, I arrived in Pierre last night. It is morning now and South Dakota is beautiful. I am leaving for your reservation by stage coach in one hour. I can't get over how much like a dream this all is. It's like I dreamed this would happen when I was a little girl or something. Michael, even the burning in my lungs has completely vanished. It was something about the journey over the Atlantic. One morning I woke up out at sea and the pain was gone. I remember your writing about the "early morning wind on the waters renewing the life spirit." Well, it happened. I will arrive at Lower Brule this evening. I'll have to give you this letter in person when I get there. Hurrah!

MICHAEL.
Nov. 11th, 1918

Dear Miss Nurse,

My whole family sits around me right now and you are with me in my heart. You are inside me and I can feel your thoughts. There is a warmth that fills my cheeks and my eyes and it feels like a fire burnin inside me.

I know you will come and see this very place someday and I will be gone. I hope you will stay cause I feel this is the place that you belong. My family is here and it doesn't matter that I won't be here.

It's just like the dream. I can hear all the victory bells ringin in my head and know you are glad. I have to go now. Daniel's callin to me from the Black Hills.

Look for me in the night sky when I am gone, I'll be east of the sun and west of the moon.

Walking Bear

CONSTANCE.
On the fourth day of the Moon of the Popping Trees "December," 1918

Dear Mother and Father,

Michael is no longer with us. His death came on the same day the war ended. I remember feeling him at my side as the bells rang out in London Square. I looked quickly to my left and could swear he was standing there beside me, sharing my joy. I believe he came to say good-bye. *(Pause.)*

I feel so alive right now, as if I've suddenly woken up from a long foggy dream which has been my life.

I am standing in South Dakota surrounded by the land he spoke so highly of. There is a vastness here that suits me. I am no longer boxed in. I can smell the wood smoke that hovers in the air. I can clearly see the sun going down on the snow-covered hill where Michael is buried.

Michael is here. His people say he is. He is here in the trees, the rocks and the water. And he is here in the great rolling plains, which, as he said, do "Look like big, long, snowy waves in the moonlight."

The Indians are poorer than I ever imagined. They all call me Miss Nurse, and I have been given a place to stay and sick people to tend to.

I am not certain of my future, but I do know I will remain here for some time. Even in death, Michael has provided me with direction.

Someday, I know you will understand why I have done this.

Your loving daughter,
Constance, "Miss Nurse"

(Music and light cue: Plaintive, possibly Native American music fades in and plays a couple of beats after Constance's last line. The stage lights slowly fade to black.)

THE END

COSTUME PLOT

CONSTANCE:
>Grey nurses uniform
>White full-body apron
>Thick white stockings
>Black socks
>Brown functional woman's boots or shoes
>White nurse's cap
>Red Cross badge or armband (optional)
>Wristwatch
>A short black cardigan sweater (buttoned at top and worn like a cape)

MICHAEL:
>Brownish/beige World War I soldier's knickers
>Long brownish/beige World War I soldier's socks
>Black or brown boots or shoes
>Sleeveless undershirt
>Button-up shirt or sweater with traditional Lakota designs/colors
>A white bandage long enough to wrap around his head many times

PROPERTY PLOT

U.S.C.: Cot, 3 pillows with white cases; 2 white sheets; small white bedside table with a clipboard, fountain pen and Michael's medical chart on it; folding chair or stool

D.S.R.: Wooden crate; piece of old-looking paper and a pencil (sharpened as if by a knife) on the crate; old-looking hardcover book

D.S.L.: Small desk or table; lantern; duplicate copy of old-looking hardcover book placed D.S.R.; metal cup for coffee or tea; envelope with Philip's letter inside; piece of writing paper; fountain pen with no ink (so as to not actually mark the paper when Constance writes; envelope containing a map and a black and white picture with wide white borders of Michael in traditional Lakota tribal clothing; cardboard box containing a blanket and a white buckskin wedding pouch (both preferably with traditional Lakota designs)

SET DESIGN

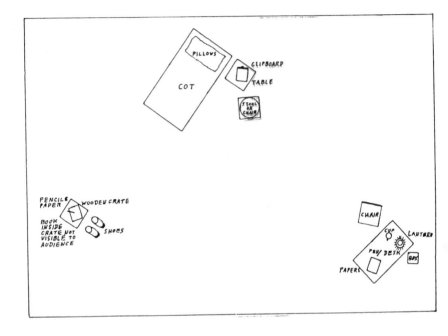

Off-Off-Broadway Festival

FOURTH SERIES
An Empty Space   Nothing Immediate   Open Admission

FIFTH SERIES
Batbrains   Me Too, Then!   "Hello, Ma!"

SIXTH SERIES
A Bench at the Edge   Seduction Duet

SEVENTH SERIES
MD 20/20   Passing Fancy

EIGHTH SERIES
Dreamboats   A Change from Routine   Auto-Erotic Misadventure

NINTH SERIES
Now Departing   Something to Eat   The Enchanted Mesa
The Dicks   Piece for an Audition

TENTH SERIES
Delta Triangle   Dispatches from Hell   Molly and James
Senior Prom   12:21 p.m.

ELEVENTH SERIES
Daddy's Home   Ghost Stories   Recensio   The Ties That Bind

TWELFTH SERIES
The Brannock Device   The Prettiest Girl in Lafayette
County   Slivovitz   Two and Twenty

THIRTEENTH SERIES
Beached   A Grave Encounter   No Problem   Reservations
for Two   Strawberry Preserves   What's a Girl to Do

FOURTEENTH SERIES
A Blind Date with Mary   Bums   Civilization and Its Mal-
contents   Do Over   Tradition 1A

FIFTEENTH SERIES
The Adventures of Captain Neato-Man   A Chance Meeting
Chateau Rene   Does This Woman Have a Name?   For
Anne   The Heartbreak Tour   The Pledge

Plays from Samuel French

SIXTEENTH SERIES
As Angels Watch   Autumn Leaves   Goods   King of the
Pekinese Yellowtail   Uranium   Way Deep   The Whole
Truth   The Winning Number

SEVENTEENTH SERIES
Correct Address   Cowboys, Indians and Waitresses   Home-
bound   The Road to Nineveh   Your Life Is a Feature Film

EIGHTEENTH SERIES
How Many to Tango?   Just Thinking   Last Exit Before
Toll   Pasquini the Magnificent   Peace in Our Time   The
Power and the Glory   Something Rotten in Denmark   Vis-
iting Oliver

NINETEENTH SERIES
Awkward Silence   Cherry Blend with Vanilla   Family
Names   Highwire   Nothing in Common   Pizza: A Love
Story   The Spelling Bee

TWENTIETH SERIES
Pavane   The Art of Dating   Snow Stars   Life Comes to
the Old Maid   The Appointment   A Winter Reunion

TWENTY-FIRST SERIES
Whoppers   Dolorosa Sanchez   At Land's End   In with
Alma   With or Without You   Murmurs   Ballycastle

TWENTY-SECOND SERIES
Brothers   This Is How It Is   Because I Wanted to Say
Tremulous   The Last Dance   For Tiger Lilies Out of Sea-
son   The Most Perfect Day

TWENTY-THIRD SERIES
The Way to Miami   Harriet Tubman Visits a Therapist
Meridan, Mississippi   Studio Portrait   It's Okay, Honey
Francis Brick Needs No Introduction

TWENTY-FOURTH SERIES
The Last Cigarette   Flight of Fancy   Physical Therapy
Nothing in the World Like It   The Price You Pay   Pearls
Ophelia   A Significant Betrayal

Recently Published One-Act Plays

THE AWARD AND OTHER PLAYS
Waren Manzi

One for the Money
Moroccan Travel Guide
The Queen of the Parting Shot
The Audition
The Award

CHERRY SODA WATER
THREE RELATED ONE-ACT PLAYS
Stephen Levi

Cherry and Little Banjo
Red Roses for My Lady
The Gulf of Crimson

CONTACT WITH THE ENEMY and GETTING IN
Frank Gilroy

DECISIONS, DECISIONS
Fred Carmichael

GENDERMAT
Mark Dunn

GUARDING THE BRIDGE
Chuck Gordon

LUNACY: A BATHROOM TRILOGY
Richard Tuttle

The Lunatic from Number Seven
Sing a Pretty Song
Search and Rescue

OFFICE SUITE
Alan Bennett

A Visit from Miss Prothero
Green Forms

Recently Published One-Act Plays

A PLACE WITH THE PIGS
Athol Fugard

POWER PLAYS

Virtual Reality
Alan Arkin

The Way of all Fish and **In and Out of the Light**
Elaine May

SERVICE
Four One-Act Plays
Karen Manno

The Spiritual Pursuit of Cosmetic Surgery
Domestic Bliss
Overeating and the Disappearing Nanny Syndrome
With a Side of Sabotage

TALES FROM THE RED ROSE INN
AND OTHER PLAYS
Don Nigro

Tales from the Red Rose Inn
Childe Rowland to the Dark Tower Came
Lucy and the Mystery of the Vine-Encrusted Mansion
Darkness Like a Dream
Joan of Arc in the Autumn
Warburton's Cook
Higgs Field
Things That Go Bump in the Night
Uncle Clete's Toad
The Malfactor's Bloody Register
Capone

UN TANGO EN LA NOCHE
Dan Hunter

PENDRAGON PLAYS

by

DON NIGRO